How
Karl Barth
Changed My Mind

Edited by
Donald K. McKim

William B. Eerdmans Publishing Company
Grand Rapids, Michigan

Library of Congress Cataloging-in-Publication Data
How Karl Barth changed my mind.
Bibliography: p. 185.
1. Barth, Karl, 1886-1968.   I. McKim, Donald K.
BX4827.B3H59   1986   230'.044'0924   86-19655

ISBN 0-8028-0099-8

To Arthur C. Cochrane
Reformed theologian, churchman, and scholar of Karl Barth with whom I first studied Barth and whose life has been a faithful witness to "the Word made flesh." With gratitude and appreciation.

Contents

Introduction

Karl Barth (1886–1968) was one of the theological giants of all time—not just of this century. He has taken his place with Augustine, Aquinas, and Calvin as a mover and shaker of the theological world. Now, one hundred years after his birth, Barth's theology continues to make an impact on the theological landscape, as did his commentary on the Book of Romans, once described as "a bomb on the playground of the theologians."[1]

The following essays are written by contemporary theologians who have been influenced in varying ways by Karl Barth. Many of them knew him first-hand and studied with him. The personal impact of Barth seemed always to make a lasting impression. Others here have read his works and learned from him through them. All have taken stock of how they have wrestled with or been shaped by Barth's theology. At many points they have appropriated his insights; at others they have expressed their reservations. But all have met Barth's mind and engaged it mightily. Taken together, the essays show how some present-day theologians are working and how they have responded to Barth's views in their various ways. The rubric used is "How Karl Barth Changed My Mind," a twist on the popular series "How I Changed My Mind" that has appeared in *The Christian Century* through the years and to which Karl Barth himself contributed three times.[2]

I am very grateful to all those who found it possible to contribute to this volume marking the centenary of Barth's birth. Others who were invited unfortunately could not participate. Sadly, one writer, William Stringfellow, died before he could complete his essay. The writers here represent diverse theological disciplines and traditions.

---

1. This comment was made by the Roman Catholic theologian Karl Adam in the June 1926 issue of the Roman Catholic monthly *Hochland* and was quoted in John McConnachie, "The Teaching of Karl Barth: A New Positive Movement in German Theology," *The Hibbert Journal* 25 (April 1927): 385-86.
2. See Karl Barth, *How I Changed My Mind,* Introduction by John D. Godsey (Richmond: John Knox Press, 1966) for these pieces.

They are a fascinating array of those whose understandings have been sharpened or shaped one way or another by Karl Barth.

Yet these are only *some* of the prominent theologians of our time who have been influenced by Barth; there are countless others throughout the world whose theology has owed much to Barth's word and thought. Recently, Dr. Nico Smith, a white man and formerly a professor of theology at the University of Stellenbosch in South Africa and now pastor of a Black Dutch Reformed Church in Mamelodi, South Africa, told of the "enormous influence" Karl Barth had on him and his attitudes about apartheid. Smith recalled a 1963 meeting in which Barth asked him, "Will you be free to preach the Gospel even if the government in your country tells you that you are preaching against the whole system?" That question made a deep impression on Dr. Smith, and subsequently helped shape his decision to leave his professorship and to live in a Black township near Pretoria.[3] For some the encounter with Barth has been dramatic. For others Barth's influence has been toward growth in different dimensions of Christian faith and life.

In addition to the contributors, I would like to thank others who have helped with this volume in special ways. I am grateful to Mr. Douglas Pierce, John Hendrickson, and Thomas Smith, student assistants at the University of Dubuque Theological Seminary, for tracking down some needed details. Mrs. Peg Saunders, our faculty secretary, did her usual expert job of typing some of the pieces. Dr. Darrell Guder, Vice-President for Academic Affairs and Dean of the Faculty at Whitworth College in Spokane, Washington, helped arrange my interview with Dr. Eberhard Busch. It was most gracious of Dr. Busch, Barth's assistant and biographer, to grant an oral interview prior to his lecturing for the Karl Barth Society of North America's Midwest Chapter meeting at Elmhurst College in November 1985. Dr. Ernest Fricke kindly aided with some translation matters in this interview. I wish especially to thank Karl Barth's two sons, Markus Barth and Christoph Barth, for contributing in the ways they did. It was my pleasure to study under Markus Barth at Pittsburgh Seminary and to welcome him to lecture at Dubuque Seminary, his first American teaching post, during this anniversary year.

---

3. See Alan Cowell, "Afrikaner Minister Tells of His Long Road of Conversion From Apartheid," *The New York Times* (November 10, 1985), p. 22. I am grateful to Dr. Deane Kemper of Gordon-Conwell Theological Seminary for alerting me to this article.

Jon Pott, Editor-in-Chief of Eerdmans Publishing Company, has been ever-gracious and supportive of this whole project. As always, I must thank my family—LindaJo, Stephen, and Karl—for their constant love and happy sharing of life together.

This book is dedicated to Dr. Arthur C. Cochrane. Dr. Cochrane is one of the foremost scholars of Karl Barth's thought in the world. He was my teacher at Pittsburgh Theological Seminary and has been my colleague at the University of Dubuque Theological Seminary. We have had many pleasant conversations about Barth and I have gained immeasurably from his knowledge and been nurtured greatly by his friendship and support. I owe him much. He has passed on to me what he also found in Karl Barth, that theology is "the joyful science"!

Donald K. McKim
University of Dubuque Theological Seminary
Epiphany, 1986

My Father: Karl Barth[1]

Markus Barth

The editor has asked me to write an appreciative characterization of my father—"a warm, human biography." If ever a son had reason to feel warm and human and appreciative about his father, I do. Why should I conceal the fact that my father always was and is the man whom I can "ask . . . and he will show" me (Deut. 32:7), a biblical father in faith and experience?

He has always been my best friend, a close comrade who reflects and encourages true attachment and true freedom. The great knowledge which he possesses, the books that he is producing, the direction he is giving to the thought and lives of many—all these ponderous gifts he has never used for exerting a formal authority over his children. He could teach us that "mother is always right, precisely when it seems to you that she is wrong," but he would make such a statement with a twinkle of the eye, and he would never make it about himself.

If I have learned anything from him in theology, it is this: that we all are fellow learners of the free grace of God, and that grace gives man a ground to live upon as a free and happy child. The secret of my father's authority is in the way in which he is under the authority of Jesus Christ.

As far as I can judge, exactly the same soft and yet irresistible impact is felt by those students and friends who have become his spiritual brothers and sons. Why should they be labeled Barthians, if the person and the teaching and a genuine understanding of Karl Barth lead directly away from religious hero-worship, political party-thinking, and speculative plotting, and toward unconditional reliance upon the freedom of grace, the freedom of theological research, and the freedom of God's children?

But let me tell something of the life of the man who is now 70 years old, and who is still working with furious energy.

1. This piece originally appeared in the *New Christian Advocate*, vol. l, no. 8 (May 1957), pp. 16-20, and is reprinted by permission.

1

He was born in a manse in Basel, Switzerland, a medieval city now largely industrialized, a city that bears the same relationship to other Swiss cities that Boston has to other places in the United States. Basel is as critical of the citizens as only the home country of a prophet can afford to be.

I did not hear it directly from my grandmother, but I have it from an otherwise reliable source, that the new-born baby asked immediately for the evening paper of May 10, 1886. When he was a first-grader, living then in Berne where his father had become a professor of New Testament and ancient church history, "Karli" showed his keen knowledge of history by volunteering for grammatical analysis the sentence, "Wellington and Blücher beat Napolean at Waterloo." He passed his school years with much reading, mainly in history, with much displeasure in arithmetic, with increasing joy in Mozart's music, with the production of astonishing dramas, and with the classical study that belongs to European education.

As a student of theology, my father displayed potent leadership in every aspect of fraternity life. In addition, the positive (that is, conservative) character of my grandfather's teaching upheld my father in many a struggle against the progressive liberalism of the first decade of this century, yet it failed to become his ultimate concern.

He went to the University of Berlin where Harnack ruled as majestic leader of liberal Christendom. My father studied under this outstanding historian and later produced a book that shocked him.

At Marburg with Herrmann and Natorp, he studied liberal theology further. Then he went to Geneva to become assistant minister to Adolf Keller. There he met, in a family belonging to the German-speaking congregation, the fervent violin student who was to become my mother.

From 1911 to 1921 my father was a minister in Safenwil, a little Swiss town with 2,000 people and one church, a strong capitalistic enterprise and a weak labor movement. Father had to preach weekly and to preside over countless meetings—from the men's club to courses in hygiene for young ladies. Here four of the five children in our family were born.

Safenwil meant for my father an endless struggle for the message that was to be the content of his sermons. He searched the books of the philosophers. He read the contemporary theological publications. As an enthusiastic "religious socialist," he helped to organize labor. He gave speeches and published flaming articles in daily papers. But above and behind all he worked on his sermons.

There was no sudden conversion when and where "it" happened: the birth or discovery of what later made Karl Barth known to the world. There was but the weekly bottleneck: Saturday night and a Sunday and usually defeat rather than victory for the preacher.

He burned much midnight oil in Bible study. Out of this he wrote the commentary on Romans, a book that, in the name of the "totally other God," seemed to say nothing but "No" to almost every theology and church work of the 19th and 20th centuries. And wasn't there reason for the "No" in the support that most university scholars and church leaders whom he respected too readily hailed and supported World War I?

Romans was read in Switzerland but it was picked up readily and reprinted again and again in post-war Germany. A positive message was heard from that book: the assertion that God is God of his own right, that his eternal word makes itself heard even now. The present collapse of idols and securities may be God's way of ushering in the kingdom of faith which is not of this world.

My father was later appointed to university chairs at Göttingen and Münster and Bonn. The strong bond between Karl Barth and Germany was sealed. Many of his closest friends and certainly all of his most enraged enemies are Germans. He has endeavored to understand, love, and enrich no nation so much as the German. And nowhere was he better understood, and also worse misinterpreted, than in Germany.

For him there was no more bitter disappointment than the turning to Hitler among some of his early friends, or the turning to a new form of liberalism, or to strongholds that resemble the fleshpots of Rome. And for him there was no greater joy than when he could tell, after a theological conference, a synodal meeting, or a discussion, that the so-called dangers of his allegedly Calvinistic and democratic theology had been overcome by some beginning of a clear and courageous confession of Christ and to the grace of God.

Germany has given him both: honors, titles, calls, responsive audiences, independent fellow-workers—and dismissal from his chair because of his disobedience of Nazi laws, slandering because of rationalism and democratism, suspicion because of alleged "red" or "pink" allures. Often the same people who had lifted him on their shield yesterday would dump him into the mud today.

He was untiring in his attack upon lazy bourgeois Christianity, on the pride of church politicians and possessive denominationalists (whether Lutheran or Neo-Calvinists), fundamental liberal and

Roman beliefs, and finally upon the nihilistic ideology and practice of the Hitler state. He was usually a lone wolf.

If there was a decisive development in his thinking between 1921 and 1935—a change from the "old" to the "new" Barth, as some have said—it came in the recognition that God, ultimately, says "Yes" to his creature.

Father saw a demonstration of the overwhelmingly positive content of the gospel. In writing his *Dogmatics,* in describing the "liberal" theologians and thinkers of the 18th and 19th centuries, in reevaluating Anselm's theological method and the 17th century's orthodox controversies, in speaking loud against the dreadful danger of Hitlerism, he made it more and more apparent that the union of God and man in Jesus Christ means the overcoming and frustration of man's revolt, and the revelation and inauguration of true humanity.

At the same time that his method and message were concentrating upon God's deed in Jesus Christ, the scope of his teaching and activity widened. Music and politics, the concerns of individual students, the ecumenical movement, travels in the central European countries, and, more than anything else, his *Church Dogmatics,* filled his days. Yet at the same time he learned to ride horseback.

Following his dismissal by Hitler, Basel gave him a chair which he still holds today after a special ruling has waived his retirement. Daily lectures and seminars, wide reading, correspondence, as well as occasional sermons in the Basel penitentiary, keep him from accepting even most urgent speaking engagements at home and abroad. Mozart's music fills his home and heart daily. Despite all pressure he is joyfully at work.

On his 70th birthday he was required to step into the limelight, but his heart is with the work he is doing, rather than with any honors that come from success. He has called for thorough restudy of political decisions. He swims against the stream of the Western reaction against Russia.

He has never felt apologetic about believing in God and being a theologian. God is God, and Christ is risen. Free grace is powerful over all mankind—this was and is his message. Trust in the full and free grace of God keeps him from compromises and makes him active.

Large sections of his books are still waiting for public discussion, and America, more than other country, has still to recover from the fantastic picture of the orthodox, whimsical, authoritarian, misanthrop Karl Barth which was spread around so long.

While a volunteer soldier in a Swiss auxiliary unit during World War II, my father learned in a new way to see, admire, and address the people who are seldom met in church. Once one of his comrades asked him, "Karli, what can you do in order not to be mixed up with that famous professor of theology, Karl Barth?" His reply was, "Well, sometimes I can do little to prevent it."

Letter to the Editor

Christoph F. Barth

Dear Mr. Editor,

Thank you, once again, for your kind invitation to contribute "in whatever way" to your memorial volume. To be honest, I am busy and I do not attach much value to anniversary manifestations, even where the person to be honored happens to be my own father "after the flesh." Yet, more than any person's honor is at stake here. Let me tell you, then, although in fragments only and using the unpretentious form of a letter, in what way I feel indebted to my father.

Living near him during more than sixty years had a decisive impact on my choice to become a theologian. I was a small boy, the third of his five children, when he served as a village pastor at Safenwil, when he wrote—and rewrote—his *Römerbrief,* while also never forgetting to fight alcoholism and capitalist exploitation which were harassing his flock at that time. Later on, as a school boy, I witnessed my father's engagement on the battlefield of academic teaching in post–World War I Germany (1921–1935). I was for some years his student when he finally had settled down in his home country, at Basel, spending now most of his time and energy on the elaboration of his *Church Dogmatics.* My own employment as a teacher of Old Testament exegesis and theology in Indonesia and in the Federal Republic of Germany meant that from 1946 on I only met my father at long intervals.

During all those years I knew him as a hard-working, passionately fighting and at times deeply troubled man, who nevertheless enjoyed life, good company, and good music and was amazingly disposable to his family. Theology—this was my conclusion from early childhood onward—must be the most joyful, the most exciting of all sciences. It was for this very simple reason that I, too, felt attracted to venture on in theology.

Doing theology—what was it all about? You might guess that being one of the sons of *this* father, I early underwent the influence of a peculiar "brand" of theology. Indeed, I learned to understand God

6

in Christ, his central revelation, and to think in a "Christocentric" way as consequently as possible. Yet there was something special in my father's search for truth that always strongly affected me. Negatively speaking, I mean his critical distance in view of everything that might be taken for granted—be it "God," religion, Christianity, inherited dogmas, or even the most cherished findings of his own reflection. Positively, I mean his awareness of the necessity or rather the chance and permission to start once again from the very beginning, as ignorant searchers, every time we venture to speak about God. Theology is a business constantly questioning itself, questioned by its own subject, or it is inevitably "bad" theology!

A second point I wish to make is in line with the first one. It concerns my father's way to read the Bible. His was an attitude of high expectancy in the face of this ancient library called Holy Scripture—a reverence and openness I will never forget. When during World War I his confidence in liberal *and* conservative theology had been shaken radically, it was not in vain that he turned to the Bible anew. What an intensity of exegetical work, beginning with two commentaries on Romans, continuing with academic courses on Corinthians, Ephesians, Colossians, and St. John, of ever-increasing importance in the biblical excursuses in the *Church Dogmatics!* What a liberty displayed at once by taking advantage of the insights of modern criticism, at another time in surpassing it by his penetrating inquiry after God's act and Word, to which biblical witnesses are pointing! What a clear-headed, natural way of understanding Old and New Testament texts as they are read in their own context! I still had to learn much about ways and deadlocks of Bible exegesis, but it was through my father's example that I discovered the Bible as a truly "interesting" book and Bible research as the very heart of theology.

This letter is already getting lengthy, but I cannot conclude it without hinting, at least, at a third point. You can hardly imagine how "secular" this giant theologian actually was. He loved the world, in spite of all its obvious misery. He read his newspaper daily and no less carefully than his Bible. He devoured classical literature, historic works, and biographies as well as fiction and crime stories until late in the night. He enjoyed traveling, watching people as they live, meeting old and making new friends. Paradoxically, he only once left Europe (his visit to the States in 1962!); he never drove a car and never owned a TV set.

One might think all this has little to do with theology. I often thought so myself. Yet the longer I knew my father, the better I understood it. There was, according to his own confession in *How I Changed My Mind,* a gradual transition from a radically "negative" toward a mainly "positive" style and accent of this theology. This change was certainly brought about by new biblical insights. But I'm inclined to presume that experiences with the factual world—to which the church of course belongs—strongly promoted it. "The world" became more and more theologically relevant through the discovery that it reflects, when seen in the light of God's intervention in the history of Israel and in the appearance of one Jewish man, its true restored identity and sometimes does so in an even more evident way than do those who are called to announce it to the world.

Let me bring this letter to an end by wishing you and your readers God's blessing for the ministry with which you are entrusted. May we all be granted new hope, new confidence, and new dedication!

Sincerely yours,
Christoph F. Barth
Basel, July 30, 1985

Memories of Karl Barth[1]

Eberhard Busch

I became interested in Karl Barth when I was a very young person. And there is a history that prepared the path I took as a child. My family was very strongly pietist. In 1925, when my father was a theology student, he told his family he wished to study at Münster where Karl Barth was a great teacher. But the whole family got very angry. The relatives said it was impossible to go to Karl Barth who, in his commentary on Romans denied the resurrection, the new life of a Christian, that God became flesh in Christ, and other things. But then my grandmother, who was a very simple but intelligent person who had only gone to school in her village and whose husband had died some years before, said, "I must find out about Karl Barth myself." So she wrote a very long letter to him in which she said she was a widow and had a son for whom she had the great wish that he should be a witness for Christ. "But now I hear from all my relatives that it is impossible to study with you," she wrote. Then she asked all these questions. Barth responded with a very long letter in which he answered all the questions and said, "I understand you very well and it is good that your son should wish to be a witness of Christ." But Barth answered in such a way that my grandmother said, "My son *must* go to Karl Barth!"

I found this letter of my grandmother's when I was an assistant and secretary in Barth's house. I was happy to see it but Barth's answer was lost during the Second World War when our house was bombed and totally destroyed. My father remained a pietistic man, with his theology obviously "corrected" by Karl Barth. Therefore when Hitler's government arose, he knew immediately what he had to do. He belonged to the Confessing Church from the beginning and when he was 28 years old he was one of the delegates at the famous Barmen Synod and voted for the Barmen Declaration. That's a long story. But it's the beginning of my interest in Karl Barth. My father

---

1. This text was written on the basis of an oral interview with Dr. Busch at Elmhurst College in November 1985—Ed.

had a picture from him in his study and when I saw it I became interested in hearing more about Barth.

I studied theology at a number of places in Germany, focusing my interests and study in Wuppertal, Göttingen, Heidelberg, and Münster. This was interesting but not satisfying. Then I read Calvin during a vacation and decided I must know more about Reformed theology. It also meant I must learn more about Karl Barth. So I decided to go to Basel; and of course this was a great decision of my life—but I saw this only in retrospect. It was a great event in my life to hear Barth's lectures and seminars. And this was greater than to read his books because he was so enthusiastic and engaging. Once I asked German theological professor Hans-Georg Geyer why he had not studied with Barth and he replied he was afraid he would be absorbed by him! It was indeed a fascinating experience to meet him personally. The young Bonhoeffer was right when he wrote after his first meeting with him in the thirties that Karl Barth was "beyond" his books, a very alive person and theologian who is so overcome by the cause of theology that he can for the sake of this matter be humble and haughty, doubting and overbearing.

In the first conversation I had with Barth, he asked me, "What do you think about my doctrine of baptism?" I answered, "It's strange to me, but I think I can follow you." Then he asked, "And what would your father have thought about this?" And I said, "He would not have agreed with you." Then Barth said, "Then you would be able to convince him." I said, "Perhaps."

I decided to do a doctoral thesis with Barth so I met with him often. At that time there was a small group of doctoral students who came to his house weekly to discuss theological problems and new books by people like Moltmann, Pannenberg, and Teilhard de Chardin. Then Barth's assistant, Charlotte von Kirschbaum, became seriously ill with atrophy of the brain. It was impossible for her to remain in the house and help Barth, so she was admitted to a hospital. Barth phoned me and said, "Now you can help me." And I said, "Yes, I will come." So from autumn 1965 until 1968 when he died, I was Barth's assistant or secretary in his house. At the beginning I was in his house for only one day a week. Then it became two and three days, so that he was very familiar to my wife and myself. He would often call and say that he was very alone and wanted me to come to speak about this or that.

In 1965 when I began, Barth was in the hospital for nearly the whole year. He was very ill and sometimes it seemed he would die.

When he returned, he was marked by his illness but his spirit was very lively. My first impression was that he was very busy at work though he suffered a long time in 1965. When I came to him, he would dictate his articles and his autobiography, which he began at this time but did not finish. He only wrote about his great-great grandfather. When he dictated letters, he was very engaged and I always felt he could see the person he wrote to in front of him. He was like an organ with many possibilities of speaking—very kind and soft but also very angry and direct. He could comfort and admonish and inform and give doctrine. He could clearly say, "Yes" or "No." He worked the whole day dictating from the early hours until nearly midnight. I had to answer many letters. Often three, four, or five books would come in a day asking for Barth's opinion. This was too much. Then sometimes he'd write a sentence on the letter saying what I should answer. Once he wrote: "Write this person a letter written in Christian *pride*." And this made good sense. Karl Barth thought that in the Christian tradition, humility was often false and that Christians were humble in a false sense. Instead, Christians should be proud—with heads held high! The message was not that *I* am a Christian and this is the reason to be proud. But Christ has risen and therefore we have the right to be proud.

In the beginning when I was in his home it was a great task to write about his life. I said, "It is interesting that this genus of literature could be converted by you." For all his life Barth said it was impossible for a Christian to write an autobiography. Then he said, "Oh, it is nothing for this genus to be converted. I always speak as the last judge about my own life and I would only justify myself. It is not possible to be really honest. There are so many biographies also written by my friends that are so many lies. So I would like to write." One day he said to me, "I think I have only some days and then I have to meet the last judge. And then he will ask me, 'Karl Barth, what have you done in your last years?' And then I would say, 'Oh, I wrote nice things about myself.' Then the last judge would be angry about me."

So, instead of being occupied by his own life, Barth became interested again in the present, especially in the changes in the Roman Catholic Church. In 1966 he made his famous trip to the Vatican and saw the Pope. In 1967 came the question of what to do with his unpublished writings. Then he gave me much material. I read the Ethics from 1928 and said how interesting that he wrote it in a Lutheran way. Barth said, "Is it so? Oh yes, it is so. But I don't like to publish these. I am not my own archivist. That is for when I have died. I have to live now in this time and not publish old things."

Then came the question, "You have written much about the ethics of reconciliation. How will you finish it?" Barth answered, "I am not quite sure that the parts of the ethics are written in the right way. When I returned from the trip to the United States, I saw I must learn much more than I know. I should study sociology, not to repeat this science, but I need to think about it more. I am not able to do this but it should be a part of this ethics. And this will also be a posthumous work. But I am not satisfied with this chapter."

Then I said to him, "How is it with the doctrine of baptism?" And Barth said, "Oh, that would be very interesting if I would finish my life on earth with this book. This is very concrete and I agree fully with what is written there." Then he opened his drawer. He said, "Here is a manuscript. Read it and tell me whether it would be interesting to publish this now." So I took it with me and in a week I read his manuscript. Then he said, "It's been eight years since I wrote this and I think there are some points where the text should be changed. Now read it once more and tell me where." So I made some marks, but he said, "It is not enough. There is more to change. Write for me some key-words to change." Then he made additions to the text and it was an amusing scene. When he dictated the text and was finished he said, "And now you are satisfied?" This was not only far better than what was given me, it was a whole other piece. But he liked to acknowledge my help.

I think this was the form in which he thought. I don't know if I can generalize about this or not. But it was my experience, and also while he was writing his *Dogmatics,* that Karl Barth needed others to give him key-words. I've spoken with other students who had the same experience. When I came to Karl Barth with serious questions about my personal life, with problems about this or that, and asked him what I should do, Barth often did not answer. He only smoked his pipe and while he was very intently listening, his answers were very short, nearly nothing. But when you went to the next lecture, even of his *Church Dogmatics,* it was full of answers to your problems. Now when you read one of his texts, you think, "Oh, this is eternal doctrine that has a sense for all time" and no one sees there are many answers to actual questions put to him. I think this was a great drive for him to write and to read his lectures. It is not coincidental that when there was not so much direct contact with students, Barth was nearly finished, he could not write much more. When he retired,

Barth wanted to finish the last volume about reconciliation but he wrote only one page. He couldn't write more.

Memories

I was impressed by how Barth was able to do things completely. When he was writing, he was only writing. When he went on vacation, he took no theology. Then he was drinking beer or wine and listening to Mozart. All that he did, he did completely and thoroughly. When there was a free hour, he didn't like to do theology—it was a free hour. I think this is the mystery of all great persons, that they can do things completely. It would be a very wrong image to think of Barth as always in the heavens of thought. He was a man who really lived with both legs on the ground. And he liked to live.

There is a very interesting story in this connection. Some days Barth took an afternoon nap. He didn't like this but because of his health he took his nap. One day when he returned from his nap he was very sad. He said to me, "Mr. Busch, I don't want to die. I don't like it." Being a young man, I was very disturbed, and thought to myself, "Karl Barth, you have written enough about this topic and you should know the right answer to your problem." But at that moment, he didn't know anything about the answer to this problem. I was hesitant to answer, but I did so in an indirect way, saying, "What do you think about Abraham? It is written about him that he died 'satisfied with life.'" And then Barth answered very angrily, "That is wrong doctrine. It is against the whole of my doctrine to say that a person can be satisfied with his own life and that now it is time to go." Then I asked, "How is it with Abraham, was he wrong?" He said, "No, that's right. But that is the judgment of later people about the finished life. So it is possible to say that even the young life of Mozart was fulfilled. But this is judged by later people. It was fulfilled because it was filled with grace."

A second remembrance. One day I came to Karl Barth and he was very nervous. I saw this and asked him what had happened. Then, as was typical for him, he said, "I had a very awful dream." And Barth had a very great sense for dreams. I asked him, "What have you dreamt?" He said, "I was dreaming that a voice asked me, 'Would you like to see hell?' And I said, 'Oh, I am very interested to see it once.'" Then a window was opened and he saw an immense desert. It was very cold, not hot. In this desert there was only one person sitting, very alone. Barth was depressed to see the loneliness. Then the window was closed and the voice said to him, "And that threatens you." So Barth was very depressed by this dream. Then he said to me, "There are people who say I have forgotten this region. I have not forgotten. I know about it more than others do. But because I know of this, therefore I must speak about Christ. I cannot speak enough about the gospel of Christ."

I close with a third remembrance. In his last year he was not so busy and I think very ill. There were some times in the spring and summer when it seemed he would die. But he survived. In the Netherlands that summer, the radio already announced that Karl Barth had died because he was so ill. But I remember the last weeks. It was the high point of the time when I lived with him. After his death, my wife said to me, "He was a little bit like an angel in his last weeks." I could also say he was like a child. He really returned a bit to his youth and very often he sang the simple songs he learned in Sunday School.

The last evening, two days before he died, I was with my wife in his house. And I think in these last times he feared the night. Therefore he didn't want us to leave his house. At one o'clock we said we'd like to go home because we had a one-hour walk. So Barth said to go when we wanted to but that he would go to his bed and that we should come and sing songs. It was 1:15 A.M. and his windows were opened facing onto the street. I said, "We'll have to close the windows because other people will be awakened by our song." Barth said, "Oh, it doesn't matter, it will be a good song." And first he began with his children's songs, then he said to take a church hymnbook and we would sing an Advent song. Now when Barth sang, he didn't like to whisper. He sang very loudly, like a lion. And I think many houses could hear his great song! Then we sang an Advent song that spoke of the great comfort that Christ is coming with his joy. And that was the last time I saw Karl Barth.

Whether Karl Barth Changed My Mind

Arthur C. Cochrane

It was the summer of 1932. I had already been baptized, confirmed, and licensed to preach. Indeed, the previous summer I had served as a student minister on a mission field at Fort William, New Brunswick, and was then serving two little country charges near Orillia, Ontario. That fall I was to begin theological studies at Knox College, Toronto. It was then—though I do not remember the day or the hour—that I read the following passage from Karl Barth's *The Word of God and the Word of Man:*

> Can a minister be saved? I would answer that with men this is impossible; but with God all things *are* possible. *God* may pluck us as a brand out of the fire. But so far as *we* know, there is no one who deserves the wrath of God more abundantly than the ministers. We may as well acknowledge that *we* are under judgment—and I mean judgment not in any spiritual, religious, or otherwise innocuous sense but in the utmost realism; Moses and Isaiah, Jeremiah and Jonah knew of a certainty why they did *not* want to enter into the preacher's situation. As a matter of fact, the church is really an impossibility. There can be no such thing as a minister. Who dares, who can, preach, knowing what preaching is? The situation of crisis in the church has not yet been impressed upon us with sufficient intensity. One wonders whether it ever will be. (p. 126)

To say that this passage changed my mind is putting it mildly. From it I learned that I had been transformed, not by myself—for that is impossible—or by any human being, least of all by Karl Barth—for that, too, is impossible—but by *God*. He plucked me as a brand from the fire of his wrath. "By the mercies of God" I was transformed ontologically and noeticly (Rom. 12:1).

That was fifty-three years ago. Over those years I have read almost everything Barth has written and much that has been written for and against him. Nothing I have read has deviated from what I read then. Of course, over the years there have been modifications, variations, explanations, and different emphases, but always the same theme. For example, in the passage quoted I heard the "Yes" of God's grace in the "No" of his terrible judgment. Later I was to hear the "No" only in the surpassing "Yes" of God's mercy. But always both together! For as Barth teaches in his doctrine of God, God is at once loving and free, gracious and holy, merciful and righteous, patient and wise.

So in 1932 my mind was changed. A change took place *within* me in that I came to know about a change that took place apart from me yet *for* me (and for all people) by God in Christ. Somewhere Barth quotes Friedrich Kohlbrügge who, when asked when he was born again, replied: "On Golgotha." And later Barth was to compose lengthy volumes of his *Church Dogmatics* to describe that Christological transformation. But let us keep to the renewal of my mind. Today we might say that I was converted, regenerated, or born again. But was this change in me effected by Karl Barth? I do not ask "How Karl Barth has changed my mind," but "*Whether* Karl Barth has changed my mind."

As far as Barth himself is concerned, I am confident that he would not claim that he had changed my mind. To be sure, three times during his life he wrote autobiographically about how he had changed his own mind. Yet he insisted that his thinking "remains at one point the same as ever. It is unchanged in this, that *not* so-called 'religion' is its object, its source, and its criterion, but rather, as far as it can be my intention, *The Word of God*. . . which is the mystery of God in his relation to man and not, and as the term 'religion' seems to imply, the mystery of man in his relation to God."[1]

We are not concerned here primarily with changes and developments in Barth's theology but with the question *how* Barth changed his mind and to some extent my mind and the minds of others. How was it possible for Barth to write as he did?

At the outset we should observe that Barth always insisted that theology is invariably a human science, a human enterprise, a fallible human work. It is a service a person renders that requires prayer, study, and reflection. The changes in Barth's mind were unquestionably the result of years of intense labor. He was his own severest critic. Since theology is a human work doubtless there were immanent factors—hereditary, intellectual, psychological, geographical,

---

1. Karl Barth, *How I Changed My Mind*, ed. John D. Godsey (Edinburgh: Saint Andrews Press, 1969), p. 37.

and historical—that contributed to the changes in Barth's thought (one thinks of World War I, the rape of Belgium, and the fact that almost all of Barth's teachers had endorsed the Kaiser's war policy).

Yet immanent factors really cannot explain the change wrought in a Moses, a Jeremiah, or a Jonah, or in a Luther, a Barth, or me, or in anyone who becomes a Christian. "With men this is impossible." It is possible only by the mystery of God whom we call the Holy Spirit who blows where he wills.

Barth has always been reticent about describing himself as possessing the Spirit or even of being an instrument, channel, or means of grace. All forms of ecclesiastical triumphalism, however subtle, were abhorrent to him. I recall a conversation I had with him in 1936 concerning the passages in Acts about the Spirit forbidding the apostles to speak the word in Asia and preventing them from going into Bithynia, while on the other hand permitting them to go into Macedonia. I asked Barth whether he believed that he had been moved by the Spirit to leave Switzerland and go to Scotland to deliver the Gifford Lectures. He replied: *Ich will keine Apostelgeschichte über mein eigenes Leben schreiben* ("I will not write an Acts of the Apostles about my own life"). He would not equate himself with an apostle. But he added: "If the Word of God is spoken and heard in Scotland, then I was led by the Spirit to come here."

I conclude, therefore, that Barth changed his mind and my mind insofar as what he taught and wrote responded and corresponded to "the one Mediator between God and man (1 Tim. 2:5), who himself directly actualizes and presents and activates and declares himself in the power of his Holy Spirit."[2]

"The Spirit blows where it wills!" We are confronted by the mystery of faith. Is it not so that we must ever say: "I believe, Lord; help Thou my unbelief"? Must we not constantly pray: "Come, Holy Spirit"? Why is it that there have been students of Barth who at first were enthralled by him and later repudiated him? Why is it that after 1945 Barth's message was eclipsed with the rise of existentialism and demythologizing? Why is it that Barth has not really had much influence in the land of Niebuhr and Tillich? Why have I not been more changed by Barth's thinking? Why did no critic of my book *Eating and Drinking With Jesus* see that I had forsaken Barth's methodology? Is it not amazing that if two people hear or read the same

2. Karl Barth, *The Christian Life: Church Dogmatics IV,4,* trans. Geoffrey W. Bromiley (Grand Rapids: Eerdmans, 1981), p. 46.

sermon or lecture, one will be grateful and rejoice, the other will be unmoved! Why is it that I have dear Jewish friends who know the Old and New Testaments better than I do and also are quite at home in Barth's *Dogmatics* and yet we cannot confess together, "Jesus is Lord"?

Perhaps the answer to these and other perplexing questions may be found in the section on "Temptation" in Barth's last book, *Evangelical Theology: An Introduction*. Temptation, he wrote, is "simply the event that God withdraws himself from the theological work of man. In this event God hides his face from the activity of the theologian, turns away from him, and denies him the presence and action of his Holy Spirit." Perhaps Barth was thinking of his own theology when he added that this withdrawal is not only a judgment upon a poor theology but also upon what from a human point of view is a good theology! May I close by quietly urging everyone to read or reread pages 133-44 of that book and ponder whether Barth has changed our minds.

Beginning with Barth

Hendrikus Berkhof

For a man like me, born in 1914 and a passionate student of theology since my seventeenth year, it was impossible to avoid the giant in my field, Karl Barth. However, when I first read him around 1931, namely his second edition of *Der Römerbrief* (1922), I had the feeling this encounter with him would also be my last one. The book disappointed me deeply. Trained in Leiden in the historical-critical approach to biblical texts, I had the impression that Barth with his rhetoric actually projected on Paul the sense of life of many postwar intellectuals in Europe. It was the same period in which Oswald Spengler (*Der Untergang des Abendlandes*, 1918) and many others wrote in the same atmosphere of "crisis." And Barth's partisans in the Netherlands were young intellectuals from the SCM circles who wanted to be both Christians and up-to-date moderns. All that made me suspicious of the biblical substance in Barth's commentary. Later I saw better how much my aversion had to do with the influence on me of both the neo-Calvinistic theology (Abraham Kuyper) and liberal theologies, both of which emphasized the link between creation and redemption, a link that was almost absent in Barth (in that period of his thinking).

Things changed around 1935 when in preparation for my doctoral examination I had to study among other handbooks of theology the first volume of Barth's *Church Dogmatics* (CD I/1). That made a tremendous impression upon me. It showed a classical breadth and depth that I had missed not only in the *Römerbrief* but also in most of the recent publications in systematic theology in general. From that moment on I read all of Barth that came my way. And I missed none of his volumes of the *Church Dogmatics*. Barth used to say he had a deep respect for all who took the time to read that voluminous work. I could reply that I was in the felicitous position that I started reading only four years after he started writing.

This intellectual discovery of Barth was superseded by the existential discovery I made two years later when my university sent me to

Berlin for the preparation of my dissertation (on the theology of Eusebius of Caesarea). Only some days after my arrival in Berlin I was introduced to the "Kirchliche Hochschule," the Seminary of the Confessing Church, at that time already a forbidden institution. There I heard teachers like Günther Dehn, Heinrich Vogel, Wilhelm Niesel, Martin Albertz, and Hans Asmussen, and preachers like Jacobi and most of all Niemöller. I took a wholehearted part in the work and the risks of the Confessing Church. So I discovered what the strictly Christocentric approach of Barth and his struggle against all forms of "natural theology" meant for them in their proclamation and resistance. I discovered the link between the Barth of the *Church Dogmatics* and of the confession of Barmen. As a result I returned to my country a convinced Barthian.

A year later (1938) I had to organize a secret meeting in Utrecht between Barth and several of his German partisans, where I met Barth for the first time. I was struck by the difference between the obscurity of most of the Germans and Barth's lucidity. In 1940 the war began and the German occupation of my country took place. As a young minister in the period between 1940 and 1945 I had no desire other than to apply in the resistance of my church all that I had learned from Barth and in Berlin.

When the war was over, Dr. Arthur Frey, an older friend of mine who was the director of the Swiss Evangelical Press Service and a close friend of Barth, offered my wife and me an attractive opportunity, after the years of occupation, to relax in the Swiss Alps. The condition was that I would write an article about the theology of Karl Barth for the *Neue Schweizer Rundschau*. When I wondered aloud why a Dutchman should carry owls to the Swiss Athens, he replied that Swiss people never believe in the greatness of a countryman unless foreigners convince them of it. So I wrote the article and we enjoyed our holidays. Frey showed the article to Karl Barth and wrote proudly to me that Barth said he had never seen such a fair and thorough article about his theological ideas and aims.

In 1948, at the first Assembly of the World Council of Churches in Amsterdam, I had another opportunity to meet Barth. There I discovered that not all of my article had pleased him. At any rate he said humorously: "According to your article I am now at the acme of my development. So I thought: What can I do now other than commit suicide?" And when we had to say goodbye, he said: "If I develop further, please be so good as to write another article about me!"

In the fifties my theological relation to Barth changed slightly. In a small book about the spiritual situation of my church[1] I blamed the Dutch Barthians and indirectly to a lesser degree also Barth, because of the formula "The Law is the form of the Gospel" and its application in the sermons. In connection with this I also objected to the neglecting of the specific work of the Holy Spirit alongside the work of Jesus Christ.

Shortly after that I wrote a small kind of "political theology" under the title *Christ and the Powers* (1953). Barth's secretary, Charlotte von Kirschbaum, was so pleased with it that she translated it and suggested Barth publish it in his series *Theologische Studien*.[2] Barth, however, refused and Frl. von Kirschbaum had to inform me, much to her regret. Some years later in a personal meeting with Barth, he began the talk with a lengthy apology for his refusal. He felt I was "mythologizing" by using and explaining Paul's language of the "powers." He could not accept such a publication under his editorship at a time when his own theology was so much under the crossfire of Bultmann and his followers. This fact did not estrange me from Barth in the least because I had never had the ambition to see this book translated. I was, however, much surprised when in Barth's posthumously published last lectures of 1962 I found in the explanation of the second petition of the Lord's Prayer an extensive treatment of "The Lordless Powers," with which I felt highly congenial. Here the school of Bultmann is no longer in view, but rather the modern scientific world that has no eye left for the mystery of the Powers. Here Barth writes that "we can speak of them only in consciously mythological terms"![3]

Quite apart from this occurrence, but in the line of my booklet of 1951, a certain estrangement from Barth took place in my theology in the fifties. At the outset I myself was not aware of it. I was just bothered by the fact that our great master restricted himself so much to his Christocentric approach that some other themes remained underexposed, mainly the work of the Holy Spirit and particularly the Spirit's relation to the realm of history. The relation Barth laid between revelation and history had always seemed unclear to me.

1. *Crisis der middenorthodoxie* (Nijkerk, 1951). For my discussion with Barth and the Barthians see mainly the chapter "Gospel and Law."

2. *Christus en de machten* (Nijkerk, 1953), ET *Christ and the Powers*, trans. John H. Yoder (Scottdale, Pa.: Herald Press, 1962). In the later English editions an "Author's Preface" reports on the adventures of the book and also on Barth's attitude.

3. *Kirchliche Dogmatik IV,4: Das christliche Leben* (Basel, 1976), ET *The Christian Life: Church Dogmatics IV,4* (Grand Rapids: Eerdmans, 1981), p. 216.

His otherwise impressive treatment of "The People of God in World History" (*CD* IV/3, §72,1) certainly did not seem to do justice to the eminent role history plays in God's revelation in Israel, in Christ, and in New Testament eschatology. In order to fill this gap (as I saw it) I wrote *Christ the Meaning of History* (1958)[4]. The book had five editions in Dutch, was translated in English and German, and finds still or anew more attention than I had expected. The interest may have to do with my attempt also to systematize the apocalyptical parts of the New Testament and to replace the still dominant fundamentalist theories by another view, more in consonance with the Christological and pneumatological center of the Christian message. I did not deal extensively with Barth in that book. Twice in the last two chapters I expressed my agreement with him. I was convinced just to go beyond the limits he had posed to himself. I wanted to complement him. Only once I criticized him slightly about his treatment of the forty days between resurrection and ascension, "in which their lack of fulfilment and their pointing to the future are not sufficiently honoured" (p. 192 n.9). At that time I was not aware of the far-reaching consequences of this criticism.

In 1964 when I was a guest lecturer at Princeton Theological Seminary, I chose as my subject "The Doctrine of the Holy Spirit."[5] In the first lecture ("The Spirit and Christ") I tried to remain faithful to Barth's Christological method. But now, as in *Christ the Meaning of History* and in other publications of that period, I tried to enlarge the outreach of this method. Following some biblical scholars, I presented the Spirit as the name for the exalted Christ in his work toward the church and the world. That offered me the opportunity to bring in the whole work of the Spirit, while maintaining a Christocentric approach. However, the consequence in the sixth lecture was a rather complicated concept of the Trinity, more a "binitarian" doctrine, which brought me under the suspicion of Sabellianism. For my identification of the exalted Christ and the Spirit I appealed to *CD* IV/2, §64,4 (pp. 322-23). I called it "a sudden widening of Barth's pneumatology" (p. 123). I was still happy with most of what Barth said. I only felt unhappy because of what he did not say and in my opinion should have said. But precisely these flaws stood in the center of my theological attention.

4. In Dutch: *Christus de zin der geschiedenis* (Nijerk, 1958), ET *Christ the Meaning of History*, trans. Lambertus Buurman (Atlanta and London: John Knox Press, 1966; repr. Grand Rapids: Baker Book House, 1979).

5. Published originally in English with the same title (Richmond: John Knox, 1964).

During and since the sixties new concerns occupied me: the historical-critical approach to the Bible, so predominant at my Leiden faculty; the "demythologizing" significance of other sciences like psychology, sociology, and evolutionary biology. My many Anglo-Saxon contacts in the World Council of Churches (of whose Central Committee I was a member for twenty years) and my frequent lecture tours around institutions of theological learning in the United States opened my eyes to the differences in approach to theology. Once or twice I lectured about "Experience on both sides of the ocean." In the same period the academic climate in Europe shifted from idealism and phenomenology to empiricism and positivism. In theology we began to look at the content of Christian faith not "from above" but "from below." When I asked Barth what he thought about the swing of the pendulum, he complained: "The 19th century comes back!" ("Das neunzehnte Jahrhundert kehrt wieder!") Barth's separation between experience and faith had meant a liberation in a time in which many of my generation were fed up with all our kinds of experience that obscured the view of the majesty and newness of the Word of God. But as a professor in the sixties I met quite another generation, hungry for experience of life in its concreteness, to whom "the Word of God" was a bloodless ghostly idea. All these influences urged me to widen my pneumatological thinking even more. If the Spirit is the bridge-builder between the Word and the world, the creator of an encounter between God and human existence, we have to prolongate not only Christology in the direction of pneumatology but also pneumatology in the direction of anthropology (and perhaps even of sociology and cosmology).

I could not agree with those Barthians for whom experience was a dirty word. I never had believed that Barth's "No!" to Brunner's "Nature and Grace" could be the last word. If the Spirit is active both in creation and in redemption, the Spirit must also be conceived as the bridge-builder between these two realms. So widening the pneumatological context in the direction of anthropology meant to me a reflection on the pneumatical meaning and use of experience.

My dogmatics handbook *Christian Faith* (1973)[6] started very un-Barthianly with a paragraph on religion and a historical-phenomenological approach to the three faith religions stemming from

6. *Christelijk Geloof. Een inleiding tot de geloofsleer* (Nijkerk, 1973), ET *Christian Faith*, trans. Sierd Woudstra (Grand Rapids: Eerdmans, 1979). The fifth Dutch edition (1985) is revised; I added a new chapter under the title "Revelation and Experience." In the forthcoming second English edition (1986) the fifth Dutch edition will be the underlying text.

Abraham. In the course of writing I discovered the centrality of the covenant-concept and as a consequence Jesus as the one obedient covenant-partner, the only true eschatological Man. "Trinity" became for me the name of the covenant-event in which God, active as Spirit, creates the new Man Jesus, who is both the receiver and the sender of the Spirit, by whose power men and women are reshaped according to the image of the true Son of God.

When I finished my book, I discovered that my pattern of thinking was widely deviating from Barth's Trinitarian and Christocentric frame. Though Barth still is the most quoted theologian in my book (in the newest edition 121 times in 528 pages), I had to give up the illusion that I was a "real Barthian."

In spite of all that, I preserved the feeling of nearness to the great master. The difference with my former period is twofold. First, I no longer see Barth as, so to speak, the final voice of the Holy Spirit for our times (as in my eyes so many staunch Barthians seem to do). Nor do I see him merely as the great prophetic opponent to all the wrong tracks of the former centuries, particularly since Schleiermacher. Like so many of his predecessors and contemporaries Barth responded to the challenges of his time. These challenges (experiences!) consciously or unconsciously played a large role in the development of his theology, especially in the years 1914–1930. It was by these very experiences that he got up against the Word of God coming from the Other Side. Yet this is not contrary to the way so many theologians after the Enlightenment had to go.

I even discovered a striking similarity with his great counterpart Schleiermacher. Both started with Anselm's "I believe in order to understand" (the motto of Schleiermacher's *Glaubenslehre*). Both stressed the reference character of the faith: to God as the transcendent Object. Both wanted to be strictly Christocentric. Both wanted to purify theology from all natural theology. Both were aware that they could and perhaps should have chosen a different method: Schleiermacher hoped that someone would come who would plan a theology on the basis of John 1:14; Barth wanted to project his dogmatics a second time not from Christ but from the Holy Spirit.

I also discovered that the struggle against natural theology is a general trend in German theology: in Kant, Schleiermacher, Hegel, Ritschl, Herrmann. Because of the rising tide of positivistic secularism, the defense against it also became more and more radical. Barth's radicality had much to do with the experiences around World War I. For these reasons Barth became for me more and more "historicized." I reread the predecessors he attacked with new eyes. I wrote my book *Two Hundred Years of Theology: Report of a Journey* in order to show the continuity in the post-Enlightenment theological themes and often also in the method and content of theology.[7]

It was from this historical viewpoint that Barth lost in uniqueness and won in strength of conviction for me. Together with his predecessors and opponents, his relentless and consistent starting from the Other Side as an answer to the embarrassments and deadlocks of all more or less experiential theology became a convincing and liberating "Copernican turn." At the same time I discovered how many questions were summoned by this turn.

I spoke about a twofold difference from my former periods. The first was the "historization" of Barth's theology. The second is related to that discovery but has to do with the individual and personal side. Theodor Siegfried, an opponent of Barth and a sharp observer of his theology, once used an image that I extend in my own way. He said that Barth in the boat of his dogmatical thinking tossing on the sea was driven by the waves to the island of the Word of God, where he could land and disembark safely. After that he put the boat back into the sea. His whole journey past Schleiermacher, Herrmann, and many others had lost its interest for him. He also forgot that after him every student of theology has to make his own journey and needs a boat for it. When the end of Barth's journey becomes for his followers an excuse not to use a boat, because a journey is no longer necessary, they inaugurate a period of Barthian scholasticism. As always in the history of doctrine, a period of great discoveries is followed by a period in which the new insights become self-evident. By being self-evident a set of spiritual convictions loses its appealing and challenging character. It becomes petrified. For new generations it loses its connections with reality. That happened to Barth's dogmatical project in the sixties. The young generations of that decade (and until now) were (and are) gluttonous for reality. They did not know what to do with words about "up there" like Barth's "the Word of God," or with Tillich's "ground of all Being" or Bultmann's "detachment from the world" *(Entweltlichung)*. Therefore the three

---

7. The book is written in German as *200 Jahre Theologie, Ein Reisebericht* (Neukirchen, 1985). In accordance with the emphasis on continuity I dealt with Bultmann and Barth under the common title "The Separation in the School of Herrmann" (chs. XIII and XIV).

great classical theologians of our era suddenly were "out," especially Barth, the most radical of the three.

Nevertheless the quest for God remained. But now God was sought in and through the realm of experience: either in the search for meaning and existence, in the desire for liberation from exploitation, in the praxis of resistance and revolution, or in the struggle for the equality of black and white, of men and women. This approach "from below" is a legitimate one, when God is a real covenant-God who fetches us down where we really are. God wants to meet us on the ways of our lives. Therefore we may start in our experiences and look for situations in which God reveals himself to us. However, when we seriously do so, we shall have the same experience as Barth did: that God meets us from beyond the limits of what we call experience. A real meeting can never be manipulated, least of all the meeting with God. Our experiential theologies are always one bridge too near. The God whom we think we meet in them is always not only but also and mainly a product of our projections and desires. This meeting sooner or later appears to be a meeting with our "self"; our "better self," but always ourselves.

I never encouraged my students to read Barth during their first academic years. That was easy advice because most of them disliked Barth and were eager to read the latest paperbacks of the "genitive-theologies." From their fourth year on, however, many stopped that reading when they discovered Barth. They had needed the boat of experience, but now they could start on new ground.

Theology is not so much a set of convictions, but a way of discoveries. We can hardly begin with Barth, but eventually we have to make our second start in him, lest our way becomes a deadlock.

Gleanings

Béla Vassady

A small reproduction of Millet's painting "The Gleaners" hangs on the wall of our living room. The harvest is over, the reapers have done their work. Three women, stooping, comb the field gathering the scattered, leftover wheat-stalks.

I had just finished the final editing on my theological autobiography,[1] in which my relationship with Karl Barth is amply described, when the invitation to contribute an essay to this volume came. So here is a cluster of memory-stalks as a result of my gleanings.

"My English is Criminal"

First scene: The First Assembly of the World Council of Churches in 1948 in Amsterdam, the Netherlands. As delegates of the Reformed Church of Hungary, my wife and I went to Amsterdam from Princeton, New Jersey, where I was serving as a guest professor at the seminary. A few months earlier, Karl Barth had visited Hungary for the second time (during his first lecture tour there in 1936, I served as his guide and interpreter). We were eager to meet him again and to hear his confidential report about the state of the Protestant churches in Hungary under a totalitarian Communist regime.

I urged him to come to the United States for a lecture tour. But he declined. "The Americans would not understand me," he said. I assured him that already during the depression of the early thirties a great interest had developed in the United States in the "theology of crisis." That interest only intensified as Barth developed his "theology of the Word." But Barth repeated, "The Americans would not understand me." Then, pausing for a second, he continued, "because I speak criminal English." I hastened to tell him that Americans were quite tolerant of foreign accents. He smiled broadly and added, "My English is criminal because I learned it by reading *detective* stories."

---

1. *Limping Along: Confessions of a Pilgrim Theologian* (Grand Rapids: Eerdmans, 1985).

27

Indeed, I recalled that in 1936, before he and his secretary boarded their train for Vienna, they bought all the detective stories available in German, French, and English, because, "After two weeks of solid theologizing, now we want to relax by reading detective stories."

Both "crisis theology" and "criminal English" belonged to the past when in 1962 Barth finally came to the United States. In Chicago and Princeton he lectured on "Evangelical Theology." This mature theology was both thoroughly evangelical and ecumenical. It was vertically "evangelical" and horizontally "ecumenical." And so was mine.

In 1973 upon my retirement, W. A. Visser 't Hooft, the first General Secretary of the World Council of Churches, wrote in a commemorative letter: "Professor Vassady [has also] helped to bring into the ecumenical movement a forceful, biblically based theology. He and I did not find it hard to understand each other, because we had both learned so much from Karl Barth."

Yet neither of us called himself a "Barthian." Why not?

A Forgiven Pietist

Scene: The library room of my "seminar" at the University of Debrecen, Hungary, in 1936. Karl Barth was in the process of delivering his lectures on "God's Gracious Election" in the assembly hall of the Reformed College. The last occasion was reserved for his answers to written questions that had accumulated during the previous days. Since they were written in Hungarian, we had to translate them into German for Barth. About six of us participated in the undertaking, which lasted for several hours. And, alas, almost everybody smoked. Some smoked cigarettes, others cigars, while Barth kept puffing away on his beloved pipe. Seeing the smoke thickening around us, he jokingly asked, "Should this smoke screen mean that we were here to produce an eclectic theology? They say in Germany," he continued, "that conservative theologians smoke cigars, liberals smoke cigarettes and Barthians smoke a pipe." Then, knowing that I never smoked, he looked at me with a twinkle in his eyes, saying, "And they also say, pietists do not smoke at all."

"Well, if that is true," I responded, "I must acknowledge that in that respect I am a pietist." "God forgives you and I too forgive you," replied Barth with a chuckle. "Of course you do," I retorted, "after all, it is written, 'Suffer the pietists to come to me for theirs is the kingdom of heaven.'" He liked to banter, even if the joke was on him.

So he added, "It is rumored that Karl Barth always starts his daily work with the same prayer: 'Lord, deliver me from the Barthians.'" Then, putting his pipeless hand on my arm, he continued, "It is good to have you as my fellow-worker in Hungary and to know that I do not need to pray, 'Lord, deliver me from the *Barthian* Professor Vassady.'"

Generic Faith and Saving Faith

At the beginning of my so-called theologian's career, I started out with a single equation: "Theology = the Sciences of Religion." Faith-experience is one-way traffic leading *from* humanity *up to* God. The sanctuary of the theological edifice (dogmatics proper) can be entered only through the vestibule (the science of religion), which in itself serves as a "Prolegomena to Dogmatics." To theologize simply means applying the methods of the various sciences of religion to Christianity as the highest manifestation of humanity's religious experience. Then the "Copernican Revolution," as it occurred in the field of theology and brought forth the whole Barthian movement, also took place in me. And in my case too it did not happen without a shaking of all preconceived foundations.

In the late twenties, the Kant Society *(Kantgesellschaft)* in Germany announced an essay contest on "The Psychology of Faith." The essay was supposed to give an empirical-analytical description of the generic process of believing as it manifests itself in humanity's personal, social, creative, and cultural life. Any leaning toward a philosophical or theological interpretation was to be avoided.

My friends prodded me to enter the competition. So I suppressed the budding theologian in me and put a tremendous amount of time and energy into the enterprise. But it was worth it because I won. However, when in the last half hour of 1929, in order to meet the deadline, I mailed my essay from a post office in Berlin, I decided: Now, for a while, I shall be reading *only* theological works and *primarily* the books of Karl Barth. So the pendulum started to swing in the opposite direction. In a few months I wrote a second book *(The Mystery of Faith)*, which turned out to be an elaborate manifestation of the triumphing theologian in me. It is still used as a standard reference work in the theological seminaries of Hungary.

The point of departure for *The Psychology of Faith* was the striving self ("I strive, therefore I am!"). It described humanity's instinctive drives and rational (spiritual) yearnings. It defined the process of generic faith in which the striving self ascertains not only its own identity, but also the identity of other beings, even that of God. On the other hand, *The Mystery of Faith*'s point of departure was the existential crisis of humanity culminating in an act of confession in the sight of its Creator and Redeemer ("I confess, therefore I am!"). By no means did it restrict itself to a sheer description of "generic faith" as *The Psychology of Faith* was obligated to do. But it jubilantly testified to God's revelation and its human concomitant, "saving faith." Paradoxically, it held up in bold relief its two basic traits: on the one hand, "saving faith" is always a whole-soul response as it acknowledges God's justice and mercy in complete humility; on the other hand, its "doer" never regards it as its own achievement but appraises and praises it as God's gracious personal gift. To be sure, in the act of "saving faith" all the psychological ingredients of "generic faith" participate. But at the same time, they are revolutionized, reoriented, and reorganized as Christian believers continue their lives and work in repentance, gratitude, hope, love, and obedience.

Together with Paul, Augustine, Luther, Calvin, and Barth, the believer is thus eager to exclaim: "I see what I can do; I do not see whence I can do it—except that I see this far . . . it is of God" (Augustine's exclamation as quoted by both Calvin and Barth). Due to these two basic traits, "saving faith" is and remains a mystery (1 Tim. 3:9).

Those who are acquainted with the theology of the aforementioned saints and particularly with Barth's theology will certainly understand when I express my indebtedness to him here. He was foremost among those who helped open up before me in the late twenties and early thirties that "strange world of the Bible" (Barth's phrase) and of evangelical theology.

At the "Barthicades"

Barricades in combat serve as shelters as well as vantage points from which to fight the enemy. The Copernican revolution in theology prompted the faculties of the Reformed Theological Seminaries in Hungary to put on the agenda for one of their annual conferences in the late thirties an in-depth discussion of Karl Barth's impact on the various theological disciplines. Present were representatives of the Comparative Religion School, but also the spokesmen of the extreme rightists (the so-called historic Calvinists) as well as the avid Barthians. No wonder the scholars' discussion soon turned into a fuselage of charges and countercharges. In anticipation of all this the pun was born: "Let us meet at the 'barthicades.' "

I was asked to lecture on "The Varied Tasks and Methods of the Sciences of Religion and of Theology," to draw the proper boundary lines between them and to answer the question, "To what extent does the Barthian movement honor the integrity of the Sciences of Religion?"

As could be expected, I found myself on the hottest spot of those "barthicades." As a psychologist who had turned into a full-fledged theologian, I had to defend the necessity and integrity of the sciences of religion and of theology and to demonstrate how a witnessing theology should and can make the best use of the bona fide findings ("empirical data") of the sciences of religion. I had to enter my caveat against the overzealous speculations of some representatives of the Comparative Religion School, but also against certain "strict historic Calvinists" who, in contrast to Calvin himself, tended to identify the gospel with their own closed doctrinal system. Finally, I also had to enter my caveat against certain extreme Barthians who disliked any psychological analyses and historical-critical comparisons.

I believed at that time, and still believe, that Barth would have never spent time and energy to write a strictly empirical psychological treatise on the varieties of religious experiences. But neither did he voice any objection when in the forties he learned that I was still publishing an empirical-psychological treatise entitled *The Incurably Religious Man*. Neither of us wanted to discard the sciences of religion; we only dethroned them as theological disciplines. At the same time we appraised and appreciated their positive contributions as "handmaidens of theology."

More Than a Mirror

Some theologians accused Karl Barth of "Christomonism." I found such a charge unjustified. However, his theology is certainly thoroughly "Christocentric." This is nowhere more relevant than in his teaching about God's gracious election (*CD* II/1-2). The Roman Catholic theologian Hans Urs von Balthasar rightly called Barth's exposition of this doctrine "the heart of Barth's theology."

Barth recognized the truth-element in Calvin's statement, "Christ is the mirror wherein we must, and without self-deception may, contemplate our own election" (*Institutes*, III.24.5). He too stressed that Jesus Christ is not merely one of the elect, he is *the* elect of God. The community of those who are elected in him is the church. The individual's election becomes effective as he or she responds to the Word of God spoken in Jesus Christ and proclaimed by the elected community.

But in Barth's theology, all this is only secondarily pertinent. His primary thesis concerning predestination is this: The mercifully righteous God (that is Christ, the Son, in oneness with the Father and the Holy Spirit) is not only the object but also the active *subject* of the eternal divine election. Prompted by free grace, he elects himself to carry out the eternal divine purpose—the salvation of humankind.

In short, as *the elected man,* Christ is the mirror of our election. But as *the electing God,* he performs a much more important role than just that of a mirror. So Barth's doctrine of predestination magnificently attests: only a consistent Christocentricity can secure and guarantee a thoroughly nonspeculative character for our theo-centric theology.

Barth's concept of God's gracious election taught me the following:

1. Never to attempt to set any limit to God's gracious activity. Our mandate is to proclaim the gospel of salvation, even to people who live as though they were rejected by God (to the intransigent reprobates) or who believe that there is no God at all (to the philo-sophical and/or militant atheists).

2. To reject any speculation in terms of the supra-, infra-, or sublapsarian theories, since God's decision in Jesus Christ occurred in "primal history," that is, in eternity.

3. To interpret divine providence only in the context of God's gracious election. Once we learned that the biggest crime ever com-mitted in human history (Jesus' crucifixion) did not take God by surprise and that it was used by God for our salvation, we shall have no difficulty in interpreting the tragic events in our own lives, in the life of our nation, and even in the life of the whole globe from the perspective of God's purposeful providence.

4. To differentiate between the instruments of God and God's voluntary agents, his bona fide servants. People who belong to the first category can vary greatly. Some of them may have no interest in God at all. Others may even fight against God. But whatever they do, God can use them all according to his inscrutable purpose. On the other hand, the agents or servants of the Lord "know whom they

have believed"; they live and act as God's elect people and their dedicated witness often turns some of his unwitting instruments into willing servants.

In 1978, after delivering a lecture in Budapest on "Predestination and Providence," I felt the discussion of the interrelationship between God's unwitting instruments and voluntary servants was a very timely subject in present day Hungary, since "the elect people of God" there must now find their bearings in the framework of an atheistic-Marxist society. What a privilege and what a responsibility they have! No wonder Karl Barth did not cease to remind them of both.

That Thicker Line

In the mid-thirties in Hungary I published an essay entitled "The Proclamation of God's Word in the Life of the Church Militant." In it I defined preaching as a twofold act, rooted and grounded *in* and thus initiated *by* the dichotomy of God's Word. Since God is both a righteous Judge and a merciful Father, God's Word entails both God's judgment and God's forgiveness. So any authentic proclamation of God's Word to the God-fleeing and God-seeking people must witness to both. I even demonstrated this in a diagram in which judgment and mercy were represented by two descending lines as they met and merged in the person who was called to proclaim to the people both sides of the total gospel.

One of my former students was studying under Barth in Basel at this time and showed him the diagram. Barth liked it but remarked, "One of those two lines, the one that represents God's mercy and forgiveness *should be drawn thicker*." And he was right. Before I learned about Barth's comment, I had already become aware that even in the dichotomy of the Word, the freely loving God makes his own judgment subservient to his mercy. Ever after I took care that Christ's invitation, "Come unto me!" should be the first and the last word in all my preaching and theologizing yet without sweeping under the rug his admonishment, "Woe unto you!"

The beachhead mission of the church, its role as a prophetic critic, should always be subordinated to its mission as a bridge, that is, as an agent of reconciliation. Without the triumph of that thicker line in one's own life and work, we could never become authentic Christians and authentic preachers.

Gypsy Band as Reminder

The seemingly limitless wheatfield in the golden sunshine of memories tempts me to go on and on in my "gleanings." But the limitations of space for this essay bid me moderation. Yet at least one more wheat-stalk still begs to be garnered.

In 1936 I ushered Karl Barth into a Hungarian restaurant in which a gypsy band was playing. Barth was so captivated by them that he almost forgot to eat. Knowing his fondness for classical music, I wondered why he was so enthralled by the Hungarian folk songs. Later I found out that as much as he liked their music, it was the theologian in him who saw in that gypsy band more than what "meets the eye" (and the ear!).

Twelve years later, in 1948, when Barth lectured in Hungary about the mandate of the church, he spoke to people in need of a compass in a post-war chaos; to people who tried to find their bearings in the midst of extreme political changes. And lo and behold, Barth illustrated what the real church should be by the gypsy band. "Look and listen—" he said,

> a really edifying spectacle that I cannot admire enough here in Hungary—how in a gipsy band every individual player has his ears and eyes glued on the leading fiddler, concentrating absolutely on the leader's improvisations, and hence playing inevitably and happily with all the others. . . . So it is in the real Church where we are confronted by a common task and dedicated to a common mission and are invited, without any moralising on the subject, to be mutually responsible for one another, to bear one another's burdens. . . .
>
> The real Church lives by being ruled by its Lord and by Him alone. It does not live according to its own discretion; neither does it live on its own responsibility and at its own risk.[2]

When in the sixties I summed up the essence of the Christ-controlled church in three inseparable statements (Christ constitutes, convokes, and confirms the church; ours is the threefold task to commune with him, to congregate in him, and to be conformed to him), I was still held spellbound by Barth's comparison. And one of his definitions of Christ's church shall always stay with me: "The Church is the living community of the living Lord Jesus Christ in the fulfillment of his existence."

Barth has often been called "the number one theologian of the

2. Karl Barth, *Against the Stream* (London: SCM Press, 1954), pp. 70, 74.

20th century." Those who knew him better would prefer rather to regard him as one of the humblest church fathers of our century, a joyful servant of Christ the Victor. Just before he died, in a telephone conversation with his lifelong friend Eduard Thurneysen, Barth finished their discussion about the gloomy situation of the world with these words, "But keep your chin up! Never mind! 'He will reign.'"[3] Barth believed this absolutely. For that reason, his company was always refreshing and the impact of his theology shall never fade.

3. "He will reign" was a saying of Christoph Blumhardt. See Eberhard Busch, *Karl Barth: His life from letters and autobiographical texts*, trans. John Bowden (Philadelphia: Fortress Press, 1976), p. 498.

The Ant and the Emperor

Paul Lehmann

Two biographers have suggested the title of this incommensurate *coram Deo* tribute of remembrance and gratitude upon the centenary of the birth of Karl Barth. Eberhard Busch, in his masterly chronicle of Barth's life and thought "from letters and autobiographical texts," refers to the "many visitors [who] found their way up there," that is, to the Bergli, taking no account of Barth's withdrawal to his favorite hideaway due to his feeling "in great need of a rest." They came "like a procession of ants," Barth wrote to his son Christoph on September 21, 1950. Yet they do not seem to have despoiled "the quietest and pleasantest holidays in living memory."[1] Since my name appears among the ants, the memory is more than a little reassuring.

My own first meeting with Karl Barth had happened in Bonn seventeen years earlier. It occurred in the course of that first fateful week following Hitler's accession to power on January 31, 1933, as then President Paul von Hindenburg invited him to form a government and become Chancellor of the Third Reich. Rumors were rife in Bonn that Barth would be dismissed before the spring semester was over. These rumors were almost confirmed. The door of the Lecture Hall of the university where Barth had been unfolding the story of Protestant Theology in the 19th Century each weekday at 7:00 A.M. bore a laconic notice that the final lecture of the semester would not be given. Barth, as it turned out, had been summoned to Berlin for a meeting with the Prussian Minister of Cultural Affairs, Bernard Rust, and the newly-appointed "Reichsbischof" of the German Evangelical Church, Ludwig Müller.

In Bonn that semester I also learned that the designation *Carolus magnus* was no longer to be confined solely to the Imperial Resident of the Palace at nearby Aachen. Another Charlemagne had come

1. Eberhard Busch, *Karl Barth: His life from letters and autobiographical texts,* trans. John Bowden (Philadelphia: Fortress Press, 1976), pp. 369-70.

upon the human scene whose royal lineage was strangely kindred to his renowned predecessor, not, indeed, by flesh and blood but by baptism and grace. Contemporaries and students of the younger *Carolus magnus* were wont to refer to Karl Barth in this way because of their awe and esteem, their indebtedness and affection that intensified as their own probing of the substance, range, and power of Barth's thought and their experience of his personal human charm developed and deepened. The phrase was a natural and grateful acknowledgment of their discovery through Barth of the excitement of theology and of their own theological formation. It expressed also an unaffected and proleptic sense of a fresh exploration under way of the Augustinian vision of the centrality of Christian faith, thought, and action for the human meaning of human life.

Dei providentia et hominum confusione was a favorite phrase of Karl Barth's. Charlemagne's biographer reports that the Emperor was accustomed to being read to at dinner. Serious books were the order of the evening ritual and special attention and pleasure was accorded to *The City of God*.[2] But, in Göttingen and Münster, in Bonn and in Basel, the tonalities evoked for those who had ears to hear clearly linked the 4th-5th, 8th-9th, and 19th-20th centuries in "a panorama of the divine economy,"[3] this time under the magisterial perceptions, passions, pertinence, and persuasiveness of the *Carolus magnus* not of Aachen but of Bonn enroute to Basel. At issue were the claims and ambiguities conjoining God with humanity or dividing humanity from God. They are the issues of ultimate loyalties and disloyalties, of ultimate trust (Luther), of the knowledge of God and/or ourselves (Calvin), of human community in concord or in conflict (Augustine).

Accordingly, in commemoration of the one hundredth anniversary of the birth of Karl Barth, the ant may be allowed a grateful homage to the Emperor by way of some account of theological formation received *lecti iuvenes, fortissima corda* (Vergil) and, in consequence, of three *notae laudationis,* briefly but *gravissima atque*

2. Einhard, *Vita Caroli,* 24. The full title is: *Vita et gesta Caroli cognomento Magni,* in Reuber Justus, *Veterum Scriptarum* (1619), pp. 1-14. ET Einhard, *The Life of Charlemagne,* trans. Samuel E. Turner, with a Foreword by Sidney Painter (Ann Arbor: University of Michigan, 1960; repr. 1972).

3. As Charles Cochrane summarizes Athanasius. See *Christianity and Classical Culture* (Oxford: Oxford University Press, 1957; repr. Magnolia, Mass.: Peter Smith, 1984).

ornatissima[4] because they are at once central to Barth's perception
and practice of Christian theology and to his continuing theological
importance; and because they happen also to be insufficiently recognized Augustinian motifs.

Of Theological Formation

As for my own theological formation, my first conversation with
Barth succinctly gathers it together. I had come to Bonn to learn from
Karl Barth what Christian theology was really about, and why. Following the protocol of those days, I sought an appointment for a
courtesy call and was received with gracious cordiality into Barth's
study. The book-lined shelves looked more like the Reference Room
of the library at Union Theological Seminary from whence I had
come than the studies of professors I had previously known. The
Patrologia Graeca et Latina, the *Corpus Reformatorum,* the
Weimarer Ausgabe, among others, lined the bookshelves and the
small passageways between. I could not suppress a comment upon
the conspicuous contrast between what I was then taking in at a
glance and what I had previously been privileged to note. To this
comment *Carolus magnus* replied with unaffected candor, a curiosity and a twinkle in his eyes, *"What* do American theologians read,
then?" What indeed!

Certainly not Karl Barth! With notable exceptions even to this
day, the Karl Barth best known in the United States is the Barth of the
second edition of the *Commentary on Romans,* supplemented by a
"Reader's Digest" approach to the *Church Dogmatics.* Emil Brunner was the principal "point of contact"—if not with God, at least
with "The Strange New World Within the Bible" and with "The
Doctrinal Task of the Reformed Churches," breaking through and
breaking up established positions and directions in Continental European theology. The tenacity of this *hauteur de silence* toward
Barth is massively evident in James Gustafson's latest exploration of
theological ethics, which finds it possible to dismiss the dynamics,
range, and complexity of Barth's lifetime of labors with the catch-
word "theological anthropocentricity."

---

4. So Cicero and Ovid described a witness who bears favorable testimony to
character in a court of justice. See *laudatio, laudator,* in Cassell's *New Latin Dictionary,* by D. P. Simpson (New York: Funk and Wagnalls, 1959), p. 339. For Vergil, see
lego, ibid., p. 341.

Careful readers of Barth will recognize, of course, the vast distortion of this reductionism, as also the dubious Edwardian coloration of an almost Islamic account of monotheism and Western culture. "What are American theologians reading, then?" Principally, the architects of American pragmatism, a theological veneer of post-Briggsian higher criticism of the Scriptures, of the optimism and corrective realism of the Social Gospel, of the evangelical liberalism of the best of German and Scottish Ritschlians transplanted to the United States, and of the bewitching "language of Canaan" designed by naturalists and ontologists of "Process Thought." These preoccupations purported to adapt for "the making of the modern mind": the covenantal discourse of mystery and revelation, myth and meaning, suffering and responsibility, history and hope. As things turned out, however, they effected the gradual displacement of the covenantal tradition by the mathematical logic of increasingly quantifiable signs generated by the cybernetic verifiabilities of science and technology. Thus, it is understandable that the heritage, habits, and *foci* of doctrinal and ethical thinking in the United States should *in principio* have marginalized Karl Barth.

To these quasi-pantheistic, polytheistic, and syncretistic preoccuptions Karl Barth alerted me and from them he delivered me. He did so above all else by identifying and exploring the dogmatic center and direction for theology and the church in a society, culture, and politics on the move. The move was *from* what Ernst Troeltsch defined as the end of Christian civilization *toward* what Richard Falk has described as a post-Westphalian world, and *for* what Dietrich Bonhoeffer has taught us to recognize as a world come of age. Troeltsch and Falk, between them, strikingly confirm Reinhold Niebuhr's brilliant aphorism that "history, like nature, never buries what it kills." Accordingly, with rare exceptions, the formative voices in American pulpits and theological seminaries—whether conservative or liberal—have nurtured generations of church members and theological students in cultivated ignorance and uncultivated innocence of a formidable dogmatic exposition and analysis of the pertinence of a theology of revelation discerned in Scripture to human believing and hoping, thinking and doing. At stake were and are the foundations and prospects of human freedom and fulfillment amid the rising barbarization of the values, purposes, and commitments that shape and sustain peoples' lives.

In raising anew and afresh the question of the centrality of dogma for faith and obedience, for the presence and responsibility of the church in the world, and, correlatively, of dogmatics as a theological discipline, Karl Barth has prepared the church for the world of today and the world for the church of today and tomorrow. This is an Augustinian achievement for which the Greeks have, once again, provided the identifying word. The word *dogma* was used by Socrates, Plato, and Euripides, among others, to denote a primary responsibility of parents toward their children. In a Greek household, this responsibility was exercised by a person whose primary task was to guide and direct the children. As a steersman or pilot *(kubernetes)* controls and guides a ship, so by metaphorical appropriation the *kubernetes* were employed to nurture the young in the *dogma,* that is, in all those matters which *one* generation (the parents) was *not* prepared to take responsibility for the next generation (the children) being *without.* Thus, *dogma*—far from identifying an arbitrary limitation imposed upon thought and action—identifies, nourishes, and sustains what it takes foundationally and focally to be and to stay human in the world.[5] Of course, there are notable and irreconcilable differences between Augustine's achievement and Barth's. Indeed, one may say of Barth's relation to Augustine what Barth once said of his own formative theological teacher, Wilhelm Herrmann: "I let Herrmann say to me something so fundamental, that carried through to its consequences, required of me afterwards to say almost everything else differently, and eventually to interpret even that completely differently than he would have done."[6]

The cardinal instance is the Trinitarian center and structure of the *Church Dogmatics,* in spite of—perhaps even on account of—the vigorous repudiation of Augustine's recourse to human psychology in expounding the mystery of the Divine Trinity. The Augustinian achievement of *Carolus magnus* neither affirms nor implies a replication of the Bishop of Hippo. But just as Augustine drew upon the authority of Scripture and upon the faith of the church as articulated in the Creeds and Councils, and unfolded a vision of the church as the center and circumference of an earthly and a heavenly human community provisionally commingled mystically and politically, so Barth draws upon Scripture and the Creeds and Councils of the

---

5. See the article on *Dogma* in Gerhard Kittel, *Theological Dictionary of the New Testament,* trans. Geoffrey W. Bromiley (Grand Rapids: Eerdmans, 1964), 2:230-32.

6. Karl Barth, *Die Theologie und die Kirche* (Munich:Christian Kaiser Verlag, 1928), p. 241. (Translation mine.) Cf. ET *Theology and the Church,* trans. Louise Pettibone Smith (New York: Harper & Row, 1962), p. 239.

church for a dogmatic-political orchestration of Charlemagne's Augustine-inspired vision of what the community of love, justice, and peace requires of the responsible exercise of power and authority in the world.

Notae Laudationis

In this sense, Barth's dogmatic-political achievement is Augustinian on the grand scale. There are, however, three notable Augustinian accents of his theological endeavors that significantly liberate theology for a world come of age. The first has to do with the relation between dogmatics and language; the second with the relation between dogmatics and humor; the third between dogmatics and political responsibility. These are the *notae laudationis* that signal a saving word for the world of today in and through the church for the world of today and tomorrow. A brief comment upon each must bring these commemorative reflections and reminiscences to a close.

1. Dogmatics and Language

Carolus magnus delivered theological language and conceptuality from bondage to propositional logic and joined them once again to poetry. This conjunction was not a surreptitious surrender to Platonism, as Bishop Nygren and German, Scottish, English, and American theologians too readily assumed. It was, instead, a dogmatic appropriation of the prophetic and parabolic witness of Scripture to God's unique way of giving himself to be known and of the responsibility of theology to know and to understand him in this way. Barth's early and too persistent critics were confused by this move, owing to their own conviction that rational coherence buttressed by scientific empirical verifiability was the surest liberation of theology from verbal and textual inerrancy. Thus it is not surprising that Barth's Christocentricity, with its patently obscurantist—and therefore specious—attempt to take the virgin birth of Jesus and his bodily resurrection with utmost theological seriousness again, should be dismissed with habitual disdain and occasional fury. As a young tutor in theology in seminary, I learned through being on the losing end of more than one fierce theological debate how intense and magisterial this repudiation of dialectical dogmatics could be. Much later, I discovered the heretical secret of this knowledgeable and zealous theological attempt to liberate orthodoxy from orthodox literalism. As with Arius before them, the trouble was that these facile repudiations of *Carolus magnus* exhibited nothing so much as the inability of their purveyors to understand a metaphor.[7] What Barth was exploring—without making a theologoumenon of theological method—was the metaphorical content and meaning of the language of dogmatics. It is this exploration which informs that epigrammatic injunction to the higher-critical interpreters of Scripture in the Preface to the second edition of the *Commentary on Romans:* "The critical historian needs to be more critical." It is this exploration which takes formal shape in the opening paragraph of the *Church Dogmatics* where the task of dogmatics is described as reflection upon the agreement between the church's language about God and the revelation of God attested in Holy Scripture. Had the recurrent *analogia fidei,* both explicitly and implicitly in Barth's interpretation of Scripture and tradition, *not* been so steadily juxtaposed to *analogia entis* by those who affirmed and rejected his thought, it might have been noticed and noted that *Carolus magnus* was actually pioneering a metaphorical interpretation of the knowledge and obedience of faith. Indeed, he himself seems not to have been fully cognizant of this creative frontier of his thought and writing. The extended sections on "Legend and Story" *(Legende und Sage)* and on "God's Time and Ours," which focused upon "The Miracle of Christmas," "The Divine Perfections," "The Angels," "Election and Ethics" are all cases in point—at least between the lines. His evocative and provocative reappropriation of the Chalcedonian *vere Deus–vere Homo* would almost certainly have brought to the surface what had been going on all around, clarified his aims, and confused his critics even more, if he had. Nevertheless, without having done so, these dogmatic labors brought him to the transforming edge of the world of today and of the church of today and tomorrow in their need and search for "an essential metaphor."

Among fellow-seekers on the right, the cordial and lively conversations in Basel and in books with Hans Urs von Balthasar over the *analogia entis* and with Hans Küng over grace and faith signaled a dawning Roman Catholic awareness of a lack of metaphorical sensitivity and humor in St. Thomas's view of both truth and conscience, a sensitivity and humor discernible through Barth's similarly structured dogmatic coherence at the service of a high doctrine of the church. As it turned out, Augustine was a partner in these conversa-

---

7. A remark about Arius in the article by Gwatkin in the Cambridge Modern History, cited by Charles Cochrane in *Christianity and Classical Culture.*

tions and discernments as he had been of Barth's search for a faithful way to think and speak about God as far back as his early friendship in Göttingen with Erich Przywara, a Jesuit (1927–1928), and with Heinrich Scholz, a philosopher in Münster (1929–1930), both of whom were devoted to Augustine, and continuing with *Ad Limina Apostolorum* after Barth's eightieth birthday in 1966. On this threshold, *Carolus magnus* cheerfully accepted his theological designation as among the *fratres sejuncti*, with the stress upon *fratres;* and there, on the way to a wonderful and memorable visit with Pope Paul VI, he impishly thought of the proverb: "Who is so smart as not to find his master in the Vatican."[8]

Among fellow-seekers on the left have been those who, having left the faith behind, strangely find themselves in the vestibule of faith and in search of a center of meaning, purpose, and hope for their lives. An unforgettable and moving instance is provided by a conundrum set down in an unpublished paper with which a friend and distinguished colleague in English Letters has favored me. The conundrum identifies exactly what the *vere Deus–vere Homo* turns out to have been and to be all about. The question is: "When is an analogy *not* an analogy?" The answer: "When it is a metaphor."[9] This search for an essential metaphor has proceeded apace and with alacrity—so much so that Hans Frei, one of the ablest interpreters of *Carolus magnus,* has found it rightly appropriate to signal a pause in "the eclipse of the biblical narrative."[10]

2. Dogmatics and Humor

The search for an essential metaphor goes on, with or without *Carolus magnus.* But just as poetry is not usually associated with Karl Barth's theology, so humor is dissociated from both his theology and his person. Nothing could be more remote from reality. Toward his metaphorically retarded critics, Barth's humor easily—and perhaps too readily—bore the bite of satire. But toward himself—which is, after all, the test case of an authentic amalgam of seriousness and

8. Karl Barth, *Ad Limina Apostolorum,* trans. Keith R. Crim (Richmond: John Knox Press, 1967), pp. 14-15.

9. Edward Lueders, *The Need for an Essential Metaphor.* Professor Lueders is currently a member of the Department of English in the University of Utah, Salt Lake City.

10. Hans Frei, *The Eclipse of Biblical Narrative. A Study in Eighteenth and Nineteenth Century Hermeneutics* (New Haven and London: Yale University Press, 1974).

humor—Barth unfailingly kept the faith. The Gideon test (Judges 9) of humor is the power and readiness to laugh at oneself. No attentive listener to sermon or lecture, no student or visitor *sans arrière pensées* could miss the twinkle in the eye, the playfulness lurking about the edges of the intensely concentrated gaze, the impish musings turned upon himself as readily as upon his contemporaries. One may add to his account of himself *ad limina apostolorum,* already noted, the instant response to the question posed in the winsome BBC film interview toward the end of his life. To the question whether he had ever desired or contemplated being other than a theologian—and if so, what?—he replied: "Not really! But if I had to choose an alternative, I should like most to be a traffic policeman!" As Barth saw it, indicating to people busily engaged in their daily tasks when to wait and when to proceed and which direction safely to take was an engrossing responsibility common in fact to a dogmatic theologian and to a traffic policeman.

Or, there is that charming comment in his "Letter to Mozart." There Barth acknowledges that Mozart has a readier access to the Divine Presence than does he. Hence he does not know whether God asks the angels to play Mozart or prefers Bach or Beethoven. Nevertheless, *Carolus magnus* ventures to think that when the angels play their chamber music among themselves, *they* play Mozart and God takes special time and pleasure to listen in.[11] I think also of a quiet evening in Barth's study in the Bruderholz Allee, 26, in 1962. He was in a mellow and retrospective mood. At one point, he remarked that sometimes he found himself wondering what the angels might think of his *Dogmatics*. This was an opening I found myself unable to pass over. So I said that I, of course, did not know what the angels might think of his *Dogmatics* but he would surely have to agree that the angels are alone among God's creatures in having the time to read it. Barth responded with a gale of spontaneous and hearty laughter—at his reverie and at himself.

3. Dogmatics and Politics

Dogmatics via metaphor and humor to political responsibility— surely this *is* theology in a new key for the church of today and tomorrow and for the world of today in search of tomorrow. It is not accidental that the memory of *der rote Pfarrer* lingered long in the

---

11. "A Letter of Thanks to Mozart" in Karl Barth, *Wolfgang Amadeus Mozart,* trans. Clarence K. Pott (Grand Rapids: Eerdmans, 1986), p. 23.

minds and hearts of some members of his parish in Safenwil. They would have been too responsive to his preaching and teaching to have been beguiled by the Reaganesque Manichaeism in our times or by the hypocritical and sentimental talk of reconciliation by Reagan and Kohl in Bitburg Cemetery. Nor is it accidental that Karl Barth should be among the very few theologians in Western Europe, Canada, or the United States who were members of Socialist parties. In addition to an astonishing number of political essays, the perceptive and proving distinction between the "law-and-order-people" and the "God of things to come" of the *Commentary on Romans*, the answer of *Carolus magnus* to Reinhold Niebuhr's haunting and reproachful *Christian Century* question gathers and focuses it all. "Why is Barth silent on Hungary?" Niebuhr accusingly asked. To which Barth responded in various times and in various ways. The substance of these responses was that as a theologian resident in a capitalist country, the primary responsibility was to note the gulf between biblical and dogmatic insights and claims, bearing upon the relations between authority, power, and justice and the practice of those relations through the structures and by the holders of power in the setting in which he lives and works. The theologian's task is to call into question the structures and practice of authority and power in the light of the scriptural and dogmatic understanding of justice as the love of God in action. The theologian's task is *not* to provide a theological warrant for the self-justification of established power and authority by howling with the wolves in the sure and certain identification of the enemy. Accordingly, it is both *beside* the point and a violation of Christian faith and obedience to cry out against Communism from the outside and on behalf of those who live under its domination and know its dehumanization only too well. By the same token, it is very much *to* the point and required of Christian faith and obedience to alert those who live under the dehumanization of capitalism and who seek to justify themselves by anti-communist fanaticism that—since they compound injustice with hypocrisy—they are in a worse case. The mote and the beam, the serpent and the dove, the sheep and the goats have never been more perceptively and politically conjoined with the poetry and politics of the Old Testament prophets, nor more faithfully applied than by Barth's deliberately chosen silence on Hungary.

The Augustinian roots of the Emperor's vision and of *Carolus magnus'* pursuit of theological existence today become concretely—and almost suddenly—contemporary. It seems, as Augustine noted in surveying his own life and times, that the Romans were once defeated in a protracted war because they loved justice for the sake of glory rather than glory for the sake of justice. "Justice, then, being absent," Augustine wrote, "what are kingdoms but great robberies? What are robberies but little kingdoms?"[12] The dialectical relation of dogmatics to politics thus enters upon a metaphorical companionship with the dialectical relation of dogma to language and to humor. Perhaps the greatest legacy of Karl Barth to the present and the future of theological thought and action is his metaphorical interpretation of the *concreteness* of dogmatic analysis and interpretation in a thematic-symphonic statement of the humanity of God for the sake of the humanization of human life in this world and the next. In focusing his search for an essential metaphor upon the Chalcedonian statement, he has provided the need for an essential metaphor with an authentic response and a warrant for a continuing companionship of discernment with wistful unbelievers of the truth of faith and the freedom of obedience that are the gospel of Jesus Christ. In so doing, he has exposed the self-effacing liberation of humor in the grace of which believers may welcome the discernment by unbelievers of the point from which the joy and peace of believing arise; and unbelievers may welcome and bear with their discovery that this is the point that believers, owing to their familiarity with the faith, are liable to miss.

Accordingly, it may be hoped that this commemorative centenary of the birth of *Carolus magnus* may document nothing so truly as the fact that Karl Barth has made it possible once again, in William Butler Yeats's haunting seeing and saying, for "the falcon to hear the falconer," for "the best (who) lack all conviction, while the worst are full of passionate intensity" to celebrate "the ceremony of innocence," and for "centuries of stony sleep" to awaken "towards Bethlehem to be born."[13]

Carole magne! Tibi Deum laudo! Requiescat in pace!

Saint Augustine's Death Day
28 August 1985

---

12. Augustine, *De civitate Dei*, IV.5.
13. William Butler Yeats, "The Second Coming," in *The Collected Poems of W. B. Yeats* (New York: Macmillan, 1951), pp. 184-85.

Rich Memories, Huge Debts

Paul S. Minear

A straight stick immersed in the still water of a pond always appears to be bent at the point of entrance. A similar optical illusion accompanies any attempt to trace the influence of one person upon another. Actual paths of influence appear to be deflected by the new medium. As retrospect replaces prospect, later developments condition all memories of an earlier time. The deeper the influence, the more difficult to trace. In probing one's own mind, one can never escape the egocentric predicament, which becomes least tractable in dealing with primal perceptions of the self and its world. My debt to Karl Barth is very real, but also highly intangible—so intangible, in fact, that only a strong sense of gratitude has induced me to share in this volume.

The passing of half a century makes it almost impossible to recall the initial impact of the Swiss theologian on American readers in the late twenties and early thirties. Perhaps my own reactions were not atypical. During that period I was completing a doctoral program in biblical studies. At the very time the pastor in Safenwil was launching his attacks on the autonomy and arrogance of liberal historicism, I was stretching every nerve to master the historical disciplines. In America those disciplines had achieved a genuine liberation from multiple forms of obscurantism and fundamentalism. So exhilarated were my friends and I by these achievements that we were inclined to resent Barth's attacks as the last futile gasp of a dogmatic biblicism. In those days it was not easy for theological systems to cross the Atlantic or to leap the wall separating dogmatics from historical studies. During my doctoral studies, so far as I can recall, I read none of Barth's works, not even his *Römerbrief,* although my field was New Testament. And when I first read them they sparked little interest and less approval. Where I lived, I could not hear the tolling of the church bell in Safenwil. And few of my friends heard it.

What was it, I now ask myself, that replaced allergy by attraction? Though memory can play tricks, several answers occur to me. One was the cumulative impact of the Depression and World War II. Not unlike the shattering influence of the First World War on Barth, this war disclosed the bankruptcy of liberal Protestantism and its reliance on historical reason. Though I was shielded from immediate personal loss, my imagination was fed daily by reading diaries, journals, and letters from Christians in prisons and concentration camps, not to mention reports of the disasters that bear the names of Dresden, Coventry, and Hiroshima. For another thing, climatic changes emerged from the work of teaching the New Testament—its story of Jesus, its claims to prophetic revelation, the testimony of the martyrs, the communal jubilation over sharing in the new creation. Increasingly the prevailing methods of study proved unable to cope with these letters and papers from prison. I was expected to teach "the strange new world within the Bible" with methods designed for the "old world," and the disparity between the worlds became almost intolerable. Moreover, professional difficulties were mild compared with personal tensions. Earlier liberation from fundamentalist doctrine was now supplanted by awareness of history-long captivities—economic exploitation, nationalistic imperialism, unceasing wars, the rule of human hearts by invisible "principalities and powers." Where could one find liberation from these rulers? Those were the years when my shelves began to fill up with books by Marx, Toynbee, Berdyayev, Unamuno, Dostoyevsky, the Niebuhrs, Brunner, Bultmann, Kierkegaard. It was in the midst of this galaxy that the star of Karl Barth began to rise in the night sky.

I began to read with mounting excitement the very books from which I had earlier turned away in distaste. For example, in *The Word of God and the Word of Man,* there is a chapter on biblical questions, insights, and vistas, every sentence of which now spoke to my condition. Now, in reading *The Epistle to the Romans* I could locate in Paul's text the origin and thrust of Barth's profound perceptions of faith in Jesus Christ. And I found that in a surprising way Barth's intellectual antagonists were my own. Intellectual friendships are often grounded in sharing the same enemies. Even after fifty years those two books exert the power to correct my reliance on prevailing methodologies and to redirect my thought to fresh recognitions of the scandal and the glory of apostolic faith. For this I am grateful.

Let me now summarize several aspects of Barth's work as a whole which over the years have compelled my admiration.

—More than any other person in this century he has restored to the vocation of "Theologian" its proper greatness and grandeur, albeit also its folly in the eyes of the world.

—More than any other dogmatic theologian of this century he has allowed his thinking on all matters to be anchored in, and prompted by, acute listening to specific biblical texts.

—In a world that, as he said, takes the nation a hundred times more seriously than it takes God, this theologian has shown what happens when God is taken a hundred times more seriously than anything else.

—In a world in which the name Christian has been falsified and trivialized, this thinker has demonstrated what happens when Jesus Christ, as the Word of God and revealer of the ultimate mystery, is allowed to redefine all the basic terms in the language of faith.

—In his exegesis of the New Testament, Professor Barth has restored to its authors their true authority as prophets and apostles, sent from the risen Christ, rather than as intellectual geniuses (to use Kierkegaard's important distinction).

—Few theologians of such stature have been able to draw upon such a vast range of metaphors and symbols; his language, like his thought, points beyond itself to the invisible source and end of all things. He even made a large place for music, though his preference for Mozart over Bach may be forgiven.

—Great respect must also be accorded for his feisty independence in the linkage of ethics to theology, whether in Hitler's Germany, in Marxist Czechoslovakia, in prosperous Switzerland, or in anticommunist America. His delight in swimming "against the stream" encouraged many other more timorous souls.

Enough space remains for a brief report on two minor incidents that deeply impressed me as characteristic of Karl Barth's mind and spirit. The first took place in 1949 when my wife and I, on our first trip to Europe, found ourselves with a free day in Basel. Summoning up a high degree of audacity I inquired whether the great man would receive me. He graciously accepted and after a few moments of casual greeting, he led the way into a vigorous discussion. Learning that I was engaged in the study of Ephesians, he turned the discussion in that direction. Not only did he know the text of the Epistle in detail; he was fascinated by the problems it posed. The question that particularly baffled him was this: In the death and exaltation of Christ did God *destroy* the principalities and powers, as some verses suggest, or did he only *subject* them to the rule of Christ, as other verses indicate? The issue, as he realized, is of very great moment. Central to an understanding of Pauline eschatology and cosmology, the issue also has decisive implications for soteriology, ecclesiology, and political ethics. I have, of course, forgotten the precise course of our exploration of the Epistle, but I have not forgotten the intensity of his interest in this ontological dimension of Paul's thought. He forced me to share his sense of the vital importance of how to visualize or to conceptualize the victory won in the Cross over all these opposing forces. The nature of that victory remains a riddle that eludes confident mastery, but it is a riddle that should elicit the best efforts of exegetes and theologians alike.

A second incident also occurred in Switzerland on the occasion of the final meeting in 1953 of the advisory commission preparing a document on the theme of the Second Assembly of the World Council of Churches, "Christ, the Hope of the World." Earlier sessions of the commission had been tumultuous and acrimonious, producing deep wounds among several of the members. This session, though less angry, had left unresolved some of the deepest issues between the more eschatological minds (e.g., E. Schlink) and the more empirical minds (e.g., R. L. Calhoun). Finally, however, the commission was able to give approval to three substantive sections of a final draft. On the last evening, when our energy was at its lowest ebb, we decided that a fourth section was needed, in order to speak more simply and directly to members of the Assembly, not as a body of professional theologians but as a group of believers; not about a technical theological problem but about the hope by which we lived. We were agreed on the desirability of such a postlude and about the general lines it should follow, but whom could we in good conscience ask to work through the night on such a task? In our desperation we turned to our colleague, and he, without a murmur, accepted the assignment. Early the next morning he presented us with his draft, reading it aloud, for there had been too little time for the mimeograph. As he read this concluding section, called "The Sum of the Matter," those who had tangled with Barth in vigorous debate could hardly believe their ears. His statement was so simple, so lucid, so free of technical jargon, so comprehensive, and so representative of the commission's work, that the commission adopted it with very few emendations, a rare thing in the life of such bodies. And when, in the following year, the report was presented to the Assembly, other sections were savagely attacked, but this work of Professor Barth's hands escaped unscathed. Ever since then, the memory of seeing how the same theologian who could conceive the complexities of the *Church Dogmatics* could also express his thought in such simple language has been an inspiration to me. One sentence from that "Sum of the Matter" applies to all of Barth's writing as well as to the Commission report:

> Among the earthly hopes of which we have spoken we must also place this one—that it may be given to those who come after us, in saying again the self-same thing, to say it differently, more clearly and more truly. . . .

One final reflection. When I drive along the Autobahn at the foot of the Swiss hill on which the Safenwil church stands, I am impelled to ponder the somber symbolism offered by the juxtaposition of two alien worlds: *Up there* the tiny village church, its quiet graveyard, green fields where cattle graze, and the parsonage where one of its pastors unearthed the dynamite in Paul's Epistle to the Romans; *down here,* almost within sling-shot range, the congested traffic of gigantic trucks and busses, bustling buildings where Japanese autos are being assembled, and all the glitter and garbage of our nomadic culture. What does each of these worlds have to say to the other? Has the gospel gained a hearing in either, in both, or in neither? With all the changes, Safenwil is still a good place to mull over the enigmatic course of Christian history since Paul wrote Romans, and to listen again to Barth's appeal in *The Word of God and the Word of Man.*

My Interaction with Karl Barth

Thomas F. Torrance

I was introduced to the study of Karl Barth in 1935 by H. R. Mackintosh, my unforgettable professor of Christian Dogmatics in Edinburgh, whose work *Types of Modern Theology, Schleiermacher to Barth* (1937) gives a fair indication of how he used to commend to us Karl Barth's "Theology of the Word of God." As soon as it appeared in 1936 I bought and read Barth's *Church Dogmatics* I/1 (translated by G. T. Thomson, who was to succeed Mackintosh in 1937 and whom I was to succeed in 1952). I was immensely exhilarated by the insight Barth gave me into the ontology and objectivity of the Word of God as God himself in his revelation, and by Barth's presentation of dogmatics as a science. But what gripped me also was his account of the Trinitarian content, structure, and dynamism of God's self-revelation as Father, Son, and Holy Spirit, expounded in terms of the biblical roots of our Christian faith and the Nicene-Constantinopolitan Creed.

When I was an undergraduate studying classical languages and philosophy at Edinburgh I read Schleiermacher's *The Christian Faith* (translated by H. R. Mackintosh and J. S. Stewart, 1928) as preparation for later study in the Faculty of Divinity. I was captivated by the architectonic form and beauty of Schleiermacher's method and his arrangement of dogmatics into a scientific system of Christian doctrine. But it was clear to me that the whole concept was wrong. Due to its fundamental presuppositions Schleiermacher's approach did not match up to the nature or content of the Christian gospel, while the propositional structure he imposed upon the Christian consciousness lacked any realist scientific objectivity. Another, more adequate way of doing what Schleiermacher had attempted was needed and I was determined from then on to make it one of my primary objectives. About the same time I probed deeply into the theology of St. Augustine, in which I found an even greater beauty and symmetry of theological form, yet in the powerful neo-Platonic ingredients of St. Augustine's thought I also found controlling presuppositions basically similar to those in Schleiermacher. I was later to hear Barth refer to Augustinian theology as *seusses Gift!*

With these convictions I began a serious study of Barth in the Faculty of Divinity. I realized that any rigorous scientific approach to Christian theology must allow actual knowledge of God, reached through his self-revelation to us in Christ and in his Spirit, to call into question all alien presuppositions and antecedently reached conceptual systems. For we must not separate from each other form and subject matter, structure and material content. By this I did not imply a rejection of philosophical thinking but rather the development of a rigorous rational epistemology governed by the nature of the object, namely, God in his self-communication to us within the structures of our human and worldly existence. In other words, the Incarnation constitutes the ontological ground of our knowledge of God and must be allowed to occupy its controlling center. But if the activity of the Holy Spirit is to be taken seriously, both divine revelation and our understanding of it must be thought out in dynamic and not in static terms. All this implied for me an exciting rethinking and deepening of the doctrine of Holy Scripture in the light of the ontology and objectivity of the Word, which is clearly lacking in fundamentalist and liberal theology alike. I found very helpful Barth's way of showing that modern liberal and fundamentalist theologies are but rationalizing variations on the ancient adoptionist and docetic heresies that kept passing over into each other in their betrayal of the gospel. Particularly enlightening, however, was the constructive way in which he developed his own distinctive evangelical position in a fresh appropriation of apostolic, classical Greek, and early conciliar theology, and of course Reformed theology, which has proved to be very relevant to our own times. The early church and the Greek fathers, Athanasius in particular, had always fascinated me, but now Barth had the effect of stimulating my study of them more than ever before.

I appreciated Barth's concept of dogmatics as a critical science in its own right, that is, as the scientific self-examination of the Christian church with respect to the content of its own proper speech about God and therefore as the critical testing of dogmas, or the church's doctrinal formulations, in the light of the *Dogma*, or the objective *Datum* of God's self-revelation. Rigorous as that concept of dogmatics as a science might be, as it was in Barth's own *Church Dogmatics,* it appeared to be little more than a formal science and fell somewhat short of what I had been seeking. But when I studied the second chapter of that half-volume on the Revelation of the Triune God, I began to find what I had been looking for in the doctrines of the *hypostatic union* between the divine and human natures in Christ and of the *consubstantial communion* between the Persons of the Holy Trinity, as well as in Barth's very impressive account of the doctrine of the Holy Spirit as the distinctive freedom of God to be present to the creature and to realize the relation of the creature to himself as its true end. Here I felt I was probing into the essential connections embodied in the material content of our knowledge of God and his relation to us in creation and redemption. I began to see that it might be possible to develop a coherent and consistent account of Christian theology as an organic whole in a rigorously scientific way in terms of its objective truth and inner logic, that is, as a dogmatic science pursued on its own ground and in its own right.

It was with this idea in mind that I went to Basel in 1937 to study with Karl Barth himself. I proposed as a thesis to work out a scientific account of Christian dogmatics from its Christological and soteriological center and in the light of its constitutive Trinitarian structure. However, Barth thought that was too ambitious for me to undertake at that stage! He asked me how else I might think of the inner connection giving coherence to the whole structure of Christian theology. When I pointed to the unique kind of connection found in *grace,* he suggested that I should examine the way in which grace came to be understood in the second century, in the period between the New Testament and the rise of classical theology. That certainly appealed to me because of my love for Patristics! It was thus that I came to write *The Doctrine of Grace in the Apostolic Fathers.* The two semesters I spent with Barth (1937-38) made an immense impact on me. I heard his lectures on the doctrine of God that were to form the content of *Church Dogmatics* II/1, studied *Church Dogmatics* II/2 (published in 1938), and engaged in intense theological discussion with him in his public and private seminars. I still believe that the *Gotteslehre* of *Church Dogmatics* II/1 and 2 is the high point of Barth's *Dogmatics.* What I have in mind is the epistemology of II/1, which must be read along with Barth's work on St. Anselm, *Fides Quaerens Intellectum;* in particular, his doctrine of God as *Being-in-his-Act* and *Act-in-his-Being,* in which he combined the Patristic emphasis upon the *Being* of God in his Acts and the Reformation emphasis upon the Acts of God in his Being. That second volume of *Church Dogmatics* surely ranks with Athanasius, *Contra*

Arianos, Augustine, *De Trinitate,* St. Thomas, *Summa Theologiae,* and Calvin, *Institutio* as a supremely great work of Christian theology.

My studies in Basel were interrupted first by a year teaching theology at Auburn, New York, and then by the war. I had gone to Auburn at the insistence of John Baillie when the chair he had once occupied there unexpectedly fell vacant. But that gave me the opportunity to think through all that I had learned and was still learning from Barth and to put it to the test in writing and delivering lectures on the whole corpus of Christian doctrine, at which I struggled day and night in order to be ready in time for my classes.

Church Dogmatics I/2 absorbed me, especially the sections on "The Incarnation of the Word" and "The Outpouring of the Holy Spirit." Here I found myself getting more deeply into the coherent structure of Christian theology under the guidance of Barth's discussion of the problem of Christology and in light of his powerful recovery of theological ontology, which had begun with *Die christliche Dogmatik im Entwurf* (1927). In particular I was gripped by the way in which he resurrected and deployed the theological couplet *anhypostasia* and *enhypostasia* to throw into sharp focus "the inner logic of grace" (as I called it) embodied in the Incarnation, with reference to which, not least as it had taken paradigmatic shape in the Virgin Birth of Jesus, we may give careful formulation to all the ways and works of God in his interaction with us in space and time. Barth had evidently taken his cue here from Heinrich Heppe's *Reformierte Dogmatik.* But this illuminating combination of *anhypostasia* and *enhypostasia* can actually be traced back to the *Contra Theodoretum* of Cyril of Alexandria. My own appropriation of this double concept confirmed and deepened my determination to work out more fully the scientific substructure of Christian dogmatics.

At the same time, I gave a course of lectures in Auburn on theology and science—not only to help elucidate the scientific nature and structure of the theology of redemption and creation, but to work out in some measure the interrelations between Christian theology and natural science and thus to begin to clear the ground for rigorous Christian dogmatics expressed within the contingent rational order with which the Creator has marvelously endowed the universe and which under God is being increasingly brought to light through our scientific inquiries. Since it is within this universe of space and time that God has revealed himself to us and his Word who is the creative Source of all rational order within it has become incarnate, I had to believe that there is a profound consonance between the intelligibilities of divine revelation and the intelligibilities of the created universe. Without taking that consonance into account I did not believe we could offer a faithful account of knowledge of God as he has actually made himself known to us.

Toward the end of that academic year (1939) I agreed to be interviewed at Princeton for possible appointment in the Department of Religion then being established at Princeton University. I believe my name had been put forward by Emil Brunner, who was lecturing at Princeton Theological Seminary that year. I recall the occasion very vividly: Theodore Green told me that they wanted someone to teach theology not as in a seminary but in an impartial, detached, dispassionate way to students drawn from all religious persuasions—Protestants, Roman Catholics, Jews—and to students of no religious persuasion at all—agnostics or even atheists. He added that "there must be no proselytizing" and asked for my reaction. I told them that I would rather teach theology as a *science!* When asked what I meant by that, I explained that in science we do not indulge in "free thinking," but are bound by the nature of the object in the field of investigation, and are committed to its objective reality and intrinsic rationality. Hence, far from thinking in some free, detached, or dispassionate way, we think as we are compelled to think by the evidential grounds, and we develop explanatory theories or laws strictly in accordance with the nature of things and their inherent rational order as they are brought to light in the course of scientific inquiry. I added that in this event I could not guarantee that no one would be converted! To my utter astonishment I found myself appointed. However, the news from Europe that June was so alarming that two days later as Brunner and I went for a walk past The Institute for Advanced Study in Princeton and discussed my hesitation about remaining in the USA if war broke out in Europe, he turned to me and said, "I think we should both return before the submarines start!" My mind was made up right away and I withdrew, very apologetically, from the appointment.

I recount this incident to indicate how committed I had already become to scientific theology and that I did not in the least feel myself at odds with what I had learned from Karl Barth. I tried to pursue the way he had opened up: with all the rational and scientific tools I could command, to cut through our ingrained self-centered patterns of thought so that we might hear God addressing us personally in his Word and at the same time attempt to set Christian theology on a sound scientific basis where the truth of God in Jesus Christ with all its compelling claims and self-evidencing force is allowed to determine how and what we are to think and say of God in ways that are worthy of him and appropriate to his transcendent rationality and grace.

I returned to Basel after the war for the summer semester of 1946, when I submitted my doctoral dissertation. Emil Brunner had agreed to lecture there while Barth was away in Bonn. Through his sons Barth asked me if I would join a small team to complete the *Church Dogmatics* should anything happen to him in Germany! How serious the proposal was I do not know. But I pointed out that it was quite unthinkable, for even Karl Barth himself never really knew how one of his new volumes of the *Dogmatics* would turn out when he embarked upon it. I recalled the fact that the *Supplementum* of the *Summa Theologiae* of St. Thomas Aquinas prepared by others had been a failure even though it was drawn from St. Thomas's own works. Fortunately, Barth was able to resume work on the *Church Dogmatics* and gave us his volumes on creation and reconciliation, though, of course, he was finally unable to complete it.

Back in Scotland I produced a work entitled *Calvin's Doctrine of Man* in order to cut through the tangled debate between Barth and Brunner on the relation between grace and nature, for in their appeals to Calvin they appeared to be shooting past each other. About the same time I began to make preparations for an English translation of the *Kirchliche Dogmatik*. However, it was only after my appointment in 1952 to the Chair of Christian Dogmatics in Edinburgh that I was in position to get matters properly organized and was able to persuade Sir Thomas Clark, the Edinburgh publisher, to invest in it. A group of capable translators came together and I was particularly fortunate to recruit Geoffrey Bromiley not only as joint editor but as our chief translator. His contribution has been as superb as it has been massive. My task was to ensure that all the translations were faithful to Barth's distinctive forms of thought and as far as possible to inject consistency into the English terminology employed. Our biggest problem was with *CD* I/2, which had to be redone several times. That was published in 1956, but it was 1969 before the fragment of *CD* IV/4 appeared, two years after it had been published in German. Geoffrey Bromiley's retranslation of *CD* I/1 was published in 1975, and the whole enterprise was completed with the Index volume in 1977.

Work on the English edition of the *Kirchliche Dogmatik* during the years when I was heavily engaged in teaching Christian dogmatic theology locked me into a sustained, intense interaction with the thought of Karl Barth in the most detailed and profound way. As I struggled with the conceptual patterns of his highly original theological exposition, I appreciated more and more the scientific and epistemological intention of his literary style and rolling periodic rhythm, even of his involved sentence structure. Behind it all lay his determination to do justice to the wholeness and manifoldness of the truth as it becomes disclosed to open relentless questioning, and his resolve not to allow his grasp or expression of it to be broken up and distorted through the imposition of logical distinctions and analytical propositions that do not represent the real connections inherent in the subject matter. This became further apparent to me when I read criticisms of Barth's argumentation, especially in *CD* I/1, advanced by logico-analytical thinkers. When I examined the German text I realized that they had been misled by the use of such logical terms as "deduce" or "infer" in G. T. Thomson's translation, which did not accurately reproduce the original text. In it Barth had studiously avoided that kind of language, for his theological conceptions were *not logically* but *ontologically* derived, in much the same way in which our basic concepts in empirico-theoretical science are derived. When I talked this over with Barth, I asked him about his references to several statements of his friend Heinrich Scholz, the philosopher of science, whom he had invited to cooperate with him in his famous Bonn seminar on the epistemology of St. Anselm. Barth assured me that he did not share Scholz's nominalist views at all, and that I had interpreted his own realist intentions rightly. Thus it became clear to me that a new translation of *CD* I/1 was needed. When that was undertaken by Geoffrey Bromiley I took care to see that more appropriate English ways of rendering the rational or conceptual connections in Barth's theology were employed.

It became evident to me that Barth was wrestling with the well-nigh intractable problem of the *subject-predicate* structure inherent in our Western grammar and logic, which others in our time have also found to obstruct and distort thought in their own fields of inquiry. For example, Bertrand Russell criticized the logical ideas of Leibniz by showing that argumentation depending on "relations" cannot be stated in subject-predicate form. This problem had already been raised early in the nineteenth century by Sir William Hamilton in Edinburgh whose doctrine of relations had such a fruitful effect in Clark Maxwell's development of the concept of the field as an independent reality. Other examples are Bertrand Russell's colleague A. N. Whitehead, who was concerned with "prehensions" in this respect, and Einstein's colleague W. M. Elsasser, who called for a "logic of inhomogeneity" in biology; or, again, in particle physics, the demand for "quantum logic" that says that the kind of subtle variable rational order actually found in the universe cannot be forced into the rigid mold of timeless logical connections. That was the point of Einstein's critique of Newton's recourse to Euclidean geometry and a logico-mechanistic system of thought, for they conflicted with what Clark Maxwell had called "real connections in nature" that, as he had already shown, require a new way of thinking in terms of continuous indivisible dynamic fields. That is, of course, precisely what Einstein developed through general relativity. This new concept of the rational structure of nature and of our scientific account of it helped me to grasp more adequately what Barth himself seemed to be after in following through the theological implications of knowledge of God as *Being in his Act* and *Act in his Being* for the interrelation of ontological and dynamic factors in our knowledge and speech of God and of his interaction with us in space and time. That is to say, Barth was already working out in theological inquiry the kind of advance in thinking that physicists were still hoping to achieve in relativity and quantum theory, in bridging the gap between the particle and the field and thus unifying their understanding of the corpuscular and undulatory theories of light.

I made a point of discussing this with Barth and suggested that although he may not have been aware of it he had in fact been operating with a form of dynamic field theory in theology similar to that which scientists had developed in their attempt to grasp the objective dynamic intelligibilities in the created universe. He was rather surprised at the correlation I had made, but accepted it. He also accepted the parallel I drew between Einstein's and his own approach to epistemological preconceptions on the ground that in theology as well as in natural science theoretical and empirical components in knowledge always operate inseparably together: the only true epistemology is that which is embodied in and is natural to the material content of knowledge. In the interest of scientific rigor in physics, Einstein had rejected Newton's way of crushing actual empirical knowledge of the world within the controlling framework of an independent, antecedently reached conceptual system, namely, Euclidean geometry. Likewise in the interest of scientific rigor in theology, Barth had rejected the practice of interpreting and formulating actual empirical knowledge of the living God within the controlling framework of an independent, antecedently reached conceptual system, namely, traditional natural theology regarded as a *praeambula fidei*. What was at stake in both instances was the demand of faithful scientific method, in accordance with which we must allow all unwarranted presuppositions and every preconceived framework to be called in question by what is actually disclosed in the course of on-going inquiry, and the need to develop an epistemological structure that is indissolubly bound up with the essential substance or positive content of knowledge. That is why Barth's epistemology is not presented in abstraction or detachment from the material content of knowledge, but in the heart of his dogmatic theology, as in *CD* II/1 where it is bound up with the doctrine of God as he has made himself known to us in space and time through Jesus Christ his incarnate Son.

I was increasingly impressed by the depth and range of Karl Barth's dogmatic theology as the part-volumes appeared, for every doctrine was subject to endless questioning in order to clarify its biblical root and determine its objective ground in God's self-revelation, and then critically tested in the light of the whole history of Christian theology and the consensus of the Fathers and Doctors of the Catholic Church in East and West throughout the ages. To interact with the *Church Dogmatics* as I had to in the process of their publication in English was an immensely enlightening and exciting experience that opened up for me the evangelical and ontological depths of the biblical message in such a profound and moving way that again and again I found myself on my knees before God in thanksgiving and adoration. At the same time it was a creative ecumenical encounter with the One Holy Catholic and Apostolic Church, with its greatest theologian for many centuries as guide and teacher. This is not to say that I did not have my own critical questions to put to the developing exposition of Barth's dogmatics—Barth deliberately provoked those questions in his students and friends, for he constantly turned the tables on his interlocutors as though they were the teachers and he the learner. Thus the questions that I found myself putting to Barth arose out of the inner substance of his theology through sharing in the movement of his thought and the growth of a deep sympathy with his mind.

In regard to the earlier volumes of *Church Dogmatics,* my chief difference with Barth relates to the element of "subordinationism" in his doctrine of the Holy Trinity, which I regard as a hangover from

Latin theology. This inevitably affects an approach to the *filioque* clause in the Western creed. I agree fully with Barth's claim that the Nicene *homoousion* applied to the doctrine of the Holy Spirit means that we cannot but trace back the historical mission of the Spirit from the incarnate Son to the eternal mission of the Spirit from the Father. But I would argue that the problem of the *filioque* was created by an incipient subordinationism in the Cappadocian doctrine of the Trinity, which the Eastern church had to answer in one way and the Western church in another way. However, if we follow the line established by Athanasius and Cyril of Alexandria, who rejected subordinationism in Trinitarian relations, we find ourselves operating on a basis where the theological division between East and West does not arise. In that event the unecumenical Western intrusion of the *filioque* clause into the Nicene-Constantinopolitan Creed simply falls away.

My other problems have to do mainly with volumes III and IV of *Church Dogmatics* and always with the question of whether Barth has been fully consistent in faithfulness to his own basic position. Through the inner correlation of creation and covenant Barth was able to offer an account of the doctrine of creation from a Christocentric perspective, in which he worked out the implications of the way in which the New Testament presents the creation as proleptically conditioned by redemption. Moreover, he was able in that way to speak of a created correspondence between God and the contingent rational order of the universe. This undercuts much of the criticism that has been leveled against Barth by those who misunderstand his rejection of an *independent* logically derived natural theology. But why did he not offer an account of creation from an overarching *Trinitarian* perspective—as was surely demanded by his doctrine of God? What then becomes of Barth's claim that the doctrine of the Trinity must be allowed to govern *all* our understanding of God's interaction with us in creation and redemption? Moreover, even if we grant to Barth that the Incarnation has the effect of giving a central place to the problem of man in dogmatics, why did he limit his account of the created order so severely to *man* in the cosmos, without very much to say about the cosmos itself except in respect of his magnificent discussions of time and providence?

Most people regard Volume IV as the high point of the *Church Dogmatics,* although Barth himself felt that the high point had been reached in Volume II. Nevertheless, *CD* IV surely constitutes the most powerful work on the doctrine of atoning reconciliation ever written. Here Barth interweaves Patristic and Reformation insights into a single fabric. Moreover, he included in it sections on the doctrines of the Holy Spirit and the church that have immense ecumencial significance. I recall him asking, in the course of his work on the second half-volume, how I thought he should answer the Roman dogma of the Assumption of Mary. In reply I suggested that he might work out more fully the implications especially of *enhypostasia* for the doctrine of the church as the body of the risen and ascended Christ, pointing out to him that unlike Calvin he had not yet given corresponding attention to a realist understanding of the church in its union with Christ. Although he may have already planned it, Barth certainly made room in subsequent sections of *CD* IV for a realist doctrine of the church along these lines.

My last discussion with Barth, which took place a few weeks before he died, was a very memorable one for me. He asked me about my concern to work out relations between theological and natural science and referred to his own lifelong stress upon the *resurrection* of Christ as the proper starting point for a scientific Christian theology. When I recalled that while some of his former students professed to agree with him in that respect, in point of fact they had developed, like Ernst Käsemann, a docetic view of the resurrection, Barth insisted that his own belief in the resurrection was quite different. Then, thumping the table, he said, *Hohl verstanden, leibliche Auferstehung!* He could not have been more emphatic about his belief in the bodily resurrection of Jesus. In that event, I said, a much closer relation between the resurrection and the Incarnation in space and time had to be thought out in our theology, to which he readily assented. I then ventured to express my qualms about his account of the ascended Jesus Christ in *CD* IV/3, in which Christ seemed to be swallowed up in the transcendent Light and Spirit of God, so that the humanity of the risen Jesus appeared to be displaced by what he called "the humanity of God" in his turning toward us. I had confessed to being astonished not to find at that point in Barth's exposition a careful account of the priestly ministry of the ascended Jesus in accordance with the teaching of the Epistle to the Hebrews about the heavenly intercession of the ascended Christ, which would have been fully consonant with Barth's anticipatory references to the high-priestly ministry of Christ in *CD* IV/1 (cf. "The Verdict of the Father") and with his persistent emphasis on the vicarious humanity of Christ. What might appear to be a "suspicion of docetism" in what Barth had written about the ascended humanity of Jesus inevitably raised questions in some quarters about how he really regarded the humanity of the pre-resurrection Jesus! I went on to add that even Hendrikus Berkhof had evidently been misled by that part-volume to advocate something like a Sabellian doctrine of the Spirit, so that eventually the doctrine of the Holy Trinity was not allowed to have its primary and constitutive place in his account of the Christian faith.

Barth was rather astonished at this reaction to what he had written and forcefully and rightly rejected any charge of docetism in his Christology. Then, with his characteristic humility, he asked me where I thought the premise lay. I pointed to the fact that, while he had given full place to the *triplex munus* of Christ as Prophet, Priest, and King, in point of fact the priestly office of Jesus Christ had been allowed to fall into the background without being fully integrated with the vicarious ministry of Christ as the obedient Son and Servant, which had its affect on his account of the ministry of the ascended Jesus Christ. I also suggested that toward the end of his dogmatics, for example in his sharp distinction in IV/4 between *Wassertaufe* and *Geisttaufe* (already rejected by Irenaeus in the second century as a form of Gnostic dualism), he had slipped back into a mode of thought that he himself had sharply rejected in earlier volumes. When at his request I traced that dualism back to *CD* IV/1, he explained that if so, it had been quite unintentional on his part, and suggested that I might rewrite those parts of *CD* IV to make them consistent with the rest of his theology!

Our discussion took us back to the point that because I had taken the Incarnation of the Son of God in space and time in the fully realist way taught by Barth himself, I felt we must think out more carefully the relation betwen our fundamental concepts in theological and natural science—and that called for a more profound thinking about the relation of the Incarnation to creation. I was encouraged by Barth's agreement with this and his blessing for my own work along these lines. He himself, he said, had not felt able to engage in that task, for it required a competence in mathematics that he did not have.

It may be worth recalling another incident in my interaction with Karl Barth. When he came to Edinburgh in 1966 to receive an honorary degree, he was accompanied by his eldest son. Markus knew of my critical attitude toward his book on baptism and wanted an *Auseinandersetzung* with me. We discussed the doctrine of baptism for nearly a whole day in the presence of his father. I argued for an understanding of baptism as the sacrament of the vicarious obedience of Christ the Servant-Son. Karl Barth himself remained silent throughout, but at the end of the day he turned to his son and said simply, *Nicht so schlecht, Markus!*

Edinburgh, Feb. 1, 1985

The Karl Barth Experience

Geoffrey W. Bromiley

It was in seminary almost fifty years ago (1937), when Barth himself was just over fifty years old, that the work of the Basel theologian first came to my attention. It may sound strange, but is nonetheless true, that although this happened in seminary, I do not recall ever hearing Barth's name in any class or seminar, or seeing any of his books on any list of recommended reading. A fellow student, however, proved to be wiser than his teachers, and incidentally referred to Barth's contribution (about which, in fact, he knew very little) at a time when the older liberalism was largely dominant, especially in the teaching of theology at Cambridge. As it turned out, the ordinary demands of the curriculum prevented me from following up the lead at once, but as soon as my final ordination and deacon's examinations were out of the way and a few weeks remained prior to my parish ministry, I embarked on an independent study of this novel Swiss thinker, beginning with some secondary works, then plunging headlong into the German *Römerbrief,* and finally working through some of the other earlier writings, both addresses and commentaries.

Three lasting impressions remain from that first and rather superficial experience of Barth. First, he helped to give me a new sense of the priorities in biblical investigation. Having studied largely under the shadow of fairly radical biblical criticism, I had shared the general feeling that meeting literary and historical objections formed a main task in Old and New Testament scholarship with a view to buttressing the authority of Scripture and strengthening the presentation of its teaching. Barth, however, made the venture of treating the exposition and understanding of the Bible as the dominant emphasis. He opened the door to theological exegesis and to biblical theology. He focused on the inner subject matter of Scripture rather than on the external circumstances. He did this, not by repudiating the historical question, but by redefining it. Truly historical study will take the Bible on its own terms, not those of the investigator. It will not try to get behind the works in order to reconstruct something else, such as a history or religion of Israel or a biography of Jesus. It will ask what these writings purport to be and do and, in thus asking, making use of the tools of literary and historical inquiry—but only as *tools*—it will find its way to authentic exposition. It will seek to enter into "the strange new world within the Bible."

Second, Barth evoked in me a heightened awareness of the relevance of historical theology. In the Anglican world of the thirties the stock of earlier theologians was at the same low point as industrial stocks. The Fathers commanded some attention, of course, and one might find individual enthusiasms for such diverse groups as the Schoolmen, the Reformers, the Carolines, and the Puritans. By and large, however, the history of doctrine, while forming an integral part of the curriculum, would often be more a source of tedium than of inspiration or instruction. Indeed, it could even become a source of irritation when some professors, with a magnificent if ill-placed confidence, preferred their own theorizings to what they seemed to regard as the gropings of an Augustine, an Anselm, or a Calvin. Barth, however, had the gift of breathing new life into these past figures, of lighting up their greatness, of bringing out their relevance to the various modern issues. Perhaps his own vital spirit, reflected in the volcanic language of *Romans,* played a crucial role in this regard. Perhaps his own genius enabled him to see in past discussions more than the participants themselves could fully realize. His use of the past might sometimes be dubious, his exposition might be a little far-fetched, and his evaluating might be slanted. Nevertheless, he brought a new dynamic, or even dynamite, to historical study, stimulating an interest in all the periods—Patristic, Medieval, Reformation, and Modern—which in my own case would have a decisive impact on future reading, teaching, and thinking.

Third, Barth won me over to an appreciation of dogmatics. My previous seminary experience had aroused no special enthusiasm for theology in this narrower sense. The biblical question, of course, had in any case claimed special attention. Moreover, the teaching of dogmatics had been somewhat less than exciting. For some teachers it seemed to consist of the more humanistic philosophizing or theorizing that Barth would so trenchantly and vigorously oppose. For others it took the form of an apologetic philosophy whose problems I had already learned to know only too well in secular classes. For others again it took the form of a somewhat pedestrian orthodoxy that lacked both inner vitality and pertinence to the pressing issues of Christian life and ministry. In contrast, Barth's approach, although obviously debatable in detail, had the obvious merits 1) of pursuing real theology, straightforward and unashamed, 2) of giving life and fire to the subject, 3) of achieving the devotional quality of prayer and praise that marks all the greater dogmaticians, and 4) of relating dogmatics not only to the intellectual questions of the era but also to the preaching ministry and all the church's work and witness. Through Barth theology became for me as for many others an imperiously demanding but also an enthralling subject, as increasing contact with the great theologians of the past, and especially the Reformers, would amply substantiate.

The next step in my Barth experience came in the busy days of parish life and involved a first immersion in the more developed Barth of the *Church Dogmatics*. The fine exposition of the Scots Confession in *The Knowledge of God and the Service of God* formed a good transition with its happy blend of historical basis and dogmatic presentation. A first reading of the German *Kirchliche Dogmatik* I/1 proved difficult, however, for time was limited, the little I had previously read of Barth had not prepared me for much of the more detailed argument, and I was not as yet so familiar with what was becoming Barth's distinctive academic style. Perhaps the simple principle that "revelation is incarnation" made the sharpest impression, for in a discussion of Barth with the then Bishop of Carlisle I used it to demolish the suggestion of no less a figure than William Temple that Barth's view of revelation eliminates the need for the Incarnation. (Barth has seldom been well known or understood in Anglican circles; the good bishop hastily changed the subject!) The following two years of doctoral study at Edinburgh, during which I explored the intricacies of German thought from the Enlightenment, by way of Herder, to the Berlin Romantics, prepared me for a better and deeper insight into Barth's concerns. In fact, however, it would be by way of the doctrine of election in *Church Dogmatics* II/2 that I would first begin to get to the heart of Barth's dogmatic enterprise. This took place when I received a first assignment on the translation team then being assembled by Thomas Torrance, and embarked on the first 200 pages of that informative and challenging if not wholly convincing presentation.

One thing led to another and in spite of a pressing round of other duties I took on the translation of the first part of III/3—the fine piece on providence—as a vacation change of pace, experimenting with the direct transmission of the German text to the English typescript as familiarity with Barth's distinctive style developed. At this time I had very little knowledge of the material in I/2, II/1, the latter parts of II/2, and III/1-2. Yet I still found Barth's treatment very helpful both for the biblical and historical discussions and for the informative and stimulating dogmatic expositions. By now, of course, critics had begun to launch attacks against the whole enterprise from various angles. Whereas some complained of the new scholasticism of Barth, others, like van Til, succeeded in finding the older liberalism, along with a vast assortment of other heresies, in the new and more sinister guise of a Reformed and evangelical theology. My own increasingly extensive and intensive immersion in *Church Dogmatics,* however, seemed to make it clear that many of the critics had not read much of Barth, or not read him carefully and scientifically enough to understand what they were reading. Barth himself would often sense that some of his readers were either failing to grasp his concerns or (intentionally) misrepresenting them.

It was when I returned to Edinburgh in the early fifties that the chance came for a far closer and broader knowledge of Barth. Already I had learned more real theology from him than from any other living teacher, so that when the chance came I could not let it slip. The problem at the time was this. Professor Torrance had collected much of the material for the next volumes of the Barth translation, but with J. K. S. Reid's departure for Leeds he needed an executive editor to work through the material, to standardize the renderings, to keep in constant touch with the publishers and printers, to correct the galleys and page proofs with himself, with Reid and T. H. L. Parker as assistants, and to prepare the indexes. My duties as minister of a fair-sized, active, and widely scattered congregation were not light, especially when accompanied by many other outside involvements in the Christian life of the city; but here was a theological task that I could hardly refuse, not for the modest financial returns, but for the enrichment that it would surely bring to the whole English-speaking church and the undoubted profit to my own thought and ministry. Thus began the great work of seeing the many volumes of the *Church Dogmatics* into print, which after some hectic years would finally find us catching up with Barth, so that in the last two volumes (IV/3 and IV/4 fragment) I used the proofs from Switzerland and was able to publish the English only a few months after the original. To round off the series we would at the end go back to the beginning, and in the light of the experience gained with the subsequent volumes I did a revision of I/1 that brought it into conformity with the whole series in style and format and from which I gained at the last a better knowledge and understanding of the important introductory discussion of the nature of theology and the doctrine of the Word of God as the Word revealed, written, and proclaimed.

My only personal contact with Barth came during this Edinburgh period. The University of Edinburgh awarded him an honorary doctorate of laws and, attended by his son Markus, he came to the city for investiture with the degree. At a luncheon held in his honor at New College Barth was in good form, making a humorous little speech in which he capitalized on his rather precarious acquaintance with English. He found it particularly amusing that as a doctor of the gospel he could now officially describe himself as a doctor of the law as well. A smaller evening gathering hosted by Dr. Torrance made possible an informative discussion of some of the issues raised by the earlier volumes, especially the problem of objectivity and subjectivity that was then so much to the fore and that agitated Barth himself so strongly in his ongoing debate with Bultmannian existentialism. A suggestion made by Torrance that Barth had yet to deal with the important biblical theme of union with Christ would provide an interesting insight into Barth's extraordinarily inventive mind when he developed the suggestion so brilliantly in the continuation of the *Church Dogmatics* in IV/3.

What can one say about the years of constant wrestling, even in linguistic detail, with the products of one of our greatest theological geniuses at the height of his powers? They obviously brought with them many frustrations and difficulties and even crises, as well as their rewards. Professor Thomson had been in seriously deteriorating health when he attempted the continuation of I/2, and at once the experience became an exasperating one when the portion he had done called for unexpectedly drastic revision. The team concept gave us an initial impetus but it also created its own problems, less sharply through the unavoidable need for editorial standardizing, more alarmingly through the failure of some team members to produce anything at all when the time was approaching for the printing of the relevant volumes. Minor trials included dealing with handwritten sheets without margins and with biblical quotations indicated only by dots. In a minor disaster a whole subsection vanished without a trace in spring cleaning, so that I had to give hasty priority to replacing it personally. The subject indexes proved to be a recurrent vexation with the need to be sure about the equivalents, the trying but necessary task of alphabetical rearrangement, and the difficulty in correlating page numbers. (The publishers in their wisdom rejected a proposal that would have proved a boon to all future scholars as well as to the editors, namely, that of including the German page numbers in the English text; as it is, readers might find it helpful to know that on average the English version saves about ten pages for every 100 pages of the original.) As a result of the various trials and tribulations and the consequent expenditure of time and energy (both nervous and physical) on secondary matters, I soon reached the conclusion that it would be quicker and easier to take on the sole responsibility myself for the translation of the later volumes (IV/1-3; IV/4 fragment; General Index). I might add that the efficient work of Reid and Parker, added to the constant help and advice of Torrance, who checked out the Latin and Greek quotations, proved invaluable, especially at the proofreading stage, both for the correction of many obvious errors (some, unfortunately, still slipped through) and also for various stylistic improvements. Parker also lightened the task with occasional humorous comments.

The translation and editing took time and effort and persistence. Yet I can hardly refrain from acknowledging what a wonderful privilege it was to be engaged in such a significant ministry. No one need be in total or even substantial agreement with Barth to appreciate the erudition, the perspicacity, the originality, and the spirituality that he so consistently displays. The writing may at times be rather heavy-handed. The sentences may be long and complicated. Some of the theses may seem to have more brilliance than cogency. The presentation may verge on hyperbole. The new perspectives may be so startling that it is hard to see at once the measure of truth that they contain. Yet those who have any real concern at all for theology and the gospel surely cannot fail to be impressed by the grandeur of the thought, the sweep of the argument, the force of the rhetoric, and the sustaining quality of the devotional commitment. Readers who have ears to hear and hearts and minds that are open to receive surely cannot fail to learn from the riches both old and new that are presented here as Barth draws so lavishly on his stores of knowledge and perception.

For my own part the ongoing experience of Barth during the years of translating the *Church Dogmatics* brought some detailed rewards in addition to the deepening and strengthening of the original impressions made by his work. On Holy Scripture, for example, Barth points the way out of the incapacitating impasse of the controversy between liberals and conservatives by setting the Bible in a comprehensive doctrine of God's Word and focusing on the unique authority of Scripture within this context instead of worrying so much about its detailed authorship and inerrancy. He can thus find a place for historical-critical work, sharply rejecting its misuse but impressing it into service in the authentic exposition of the text that we need if we are to hear God's Word in and through the biblical words. He need not waste his energies on an apologetic defense of Scripture against alleged errors and contradictions, for Scripture can take care of itself. He rescues the Bible from both pontificating church leaders on the one side and authoritarian scholars on the other, letting it have its own say in order that we may be told God's Word through it. He opens the door to genuine obedience to Scripture by concentrating on the dynamic role of the Spirit as the one who, having given the biblical witness, does not abandon it, but comes in living power, so that its voice is in very truth the voice of God. Barth's doctrine raises its own problems both on the right hand and on the left, yet by his emphasis on the Bible's authority, his grounding of this authority in God, his linking of the divine Word and the human word and his confidence in the power of the Bible, Barth offers suggestions that might help the church to move on from endless disputes about Scripture and the related weakening of its functional primacy to a more positive and fruitful use that will manifest itself in a better obedience of life and ministry.

In theology, Barth has rendered a twofold service. First, he has called theology back to its proper object in God and given it a more truly scientific basis under the control of this object, who is always also its subject. In so doing he has restored to theology its integrity as an academic discipline in its own right that need not disguise itself among the humanities. But second, he has also related theology firmly to the church's mission. Theology for Barth is no mere academic exercise. It does not serve only to satisfy intellectual needs or to provide apologetic arguments. It brings the whole life and proclamation of the church under scrutiny, subjecting them to testing by the biblical norm, pointing out the need for addition, correction, or subtraction as the church lives out the Christian life and proclaims the Christian message in the diverse cultures and shifting circumstances of the world. In this sense Barth treats theology itself as a form of ministry, for its scrutinizing is not an exercise in domination but an act of service that protects the church against error and secularization, that helps it to achieve a purity of teaching and preaching, and that first and supremely and continuously theology must also render in exemplary fashion to itself.

As regards the doctrine of God, the incarnational theme of God's secondary objectivity and the related reconstruction of the understanding of analogy have been particularly helpful as threads to guide us through the labyrinth of modern epistemological discussion. In the account of the divine perfections, Barth's statements on omnipotence, omniscience, and omnipresence (with the associated remarks on omnivolence and omnicausality) should also be noted, for Barth refuses to let these qualities become abstractions to which God himself is subject, but relates them strictly to God in a way that preserves for God his own free choice in their exercise. Thus Barth avoids what might seem theoretically to be the necessary dualism between God's omnipotence and the impotence of the cross, for, as he understands it, God may be powerful even in the form of apparent weakness. Similarly, the power of God forms the sure basis rather than the negation of authentic human power (as distinct from the inauthentic power of rebellious self-assertion). A striking contribution in connection with the perfection of divine glory is Barth's affirmation of the beauty of God and the call for a corresponding beauty in our theological endeavors—and also, one might add, in the worship of God and the whole of Christian life and character. In this recognition of the divine beauty Barth catches a note that has too seldom been heard in more abstruse and often stylistically inferior theological deliberations. To read the passage is an integral part of the deeper Barth experience that no one who sets out to be a real theologian or a faithful witness to Christ should on any account miss.

In the matter of creation, in which Barth has never enjoyed too high a reputation, he surely merits our thanks for sticking to his theological task and resisting entanglement in the tiresome conflicts of science and religion. His theological instinct has not betrayed him in directing attention primarily to the covenant purpose of God, at least for the human creature, and hence to the essential relation between creation and covenant. The prior orientation of the covenant to Christ gives an additional Christological slant to creation and makes possible a confident assertion of the essential goodness of creation even though Barth can wax merry at the expense of theodicies that lack the necessary Christological basis or cornerstone. His reconsideration of the *imago dei* in the light of our essential being in relationship may not exhaust the meaning of this pregnant biblical concept, but it sets in relief an element that undoubtedly belongs to both divine and human life and will thus claim a place in all future discussion. The plea for a theological anthropology has special relevance at a time when even theologians have attached so much value to secular anthropologies either in competition or in cooperation with the biblical data; and here again the focus on Christ, this time in his fourfold relation to God, others, self, and time, makes for a stimulating presentation that prepares the ground both for the ethics of creation and for the doctrine of sin and reconciliation. Barth can also take angels so seriously that he devotes a whole section to them within the doctrine of God's providential care for creation, and if his account of evil fails to bring complete satisfaction it does at least make the implicit suggestion that evil, being irrational by nature, does not permit any fully rational exposition or explanation.

Richest of all in insights, perhaps, are the massive volumes on reconciliation, from which few readers can fail to derive some profit even if they have to be critical of many of the theses. For my own part, I found particular help in the close interweaving of Christ's person and work, the handling of the so-called *kenosis* of Christ, the notable stress on the objective reality of Christ's vicarious life, death, and resurrection, the exploration of the depths of sin in antithesis to Christ's priestly, kingly, and prophetic ministry, the fine discussion of justification and sanctification, the tight relating of conversion and calling, and the many insights regarding the gathering, upbuilding, and sending of the community. Unforgettable, too, are the many biblical expositions, whether of Old Testament incidents, or of such key passages as John 3:16 or 2 Corinthians 5:18ff., or of great chapters such as Paul's hymn to love in 1 Corinthians 13. Here also, as everywhere in the *Church Dogmatics,* exciting historical presentations offer new perspectives on doctrinal and ecclesiastical developments, both commendable and debatable. One might mention the excursus on covenant theology (IV/1) by way of example.

The completion of the *Church Dogmatics*—if one can call a fragment complete—meant that for some years, except for work on the General Index, my active contact with Barth had to take the form of rather frustrating elective courses and seminars. I say frustrating because the sheer weight of the material tended to overwhelm students. Attempts to isolate specific themes ran up against the difficulty that in Barth it is virtually impossible to see one thing except in the light of everything else. Thus, satisfying evaluation and interaction, whether in general or in detail, proved very hard to achieve and the secondary studies were not always helpful. It was with these problems that I finally wrote my own little introduction *The*

Theology of Karl Barth, not in the vain hope of giving a full account, let alone engaging in comprehensive exposition, evaluation, or exploration of the ramifications, but with the very practical aim of enabling students to get a reliable enough grasp of the general content and thrust of the *Church Dogmatics* to know what they were talking about when dealing intensively and at first hand with one or other of the parts. Those who are well versed in the series will, I am sure, excuse the many gaps and imperfections when they remember how many of Barth's pages—often well packed—have to go into a single page of a work of this kind, yet also how impossible it is for the average student to follow the counsel of perfection and read the whole of *Church Dogmatics* in person. At least the references are there so that those who are interested may check out Barth's own far richer presentation for themselves. It is also a hope that some may be inspired by this little nibble to tackle a full course or even the whole meal for themselves when they have the time to do so.

The flood of new materials released by the project of a *Gesamtausgabe* of Barth's works brought a new demand for translation in the late seventies and early eighties and I thus saw myself plunged into a new phase, or two new phases, of the Barth experience, with some early works on the one side and such later works as *The Christian Life* and the 1961-1968 *Letters* on the other. I found the early pieces especially instructive for the light they shed on the development of Barth from the author of the *Römerbrief* to the author of the *Church Dogmatics.* The Barth/Bultmann *Letters* give evidence of the cracks that were present from the very first in the apparent alliance with Bultmann: Barth's insistence on exegesis *with* the biblical authors instead of *about* them; his refusal to bow to the primacy of existentialism and its supposedly purer concepts; his concern for the facticity of the revealing and reconciling word and work of God in Christ; his associated conviction that God's work *in* us can rest only on the work that he has already accomplished *for* us and his demand for a stronger stand against the oath of personal loyalty that was being imposed by Hitler. His lectures on Schleiermacher *(The Theology of Schleiermacher)* supply us with the full-scale examination that underlies the various Schleiermacher essays and explains Barth's rejection of the whole Schleiermacher tradition in spite of his continuing admiration for this great theologian and the nagging doubt whether after all it might not be possible to take him in better part. The Münster *John Lectures,* especially the long exposition of John 1, bring before us many of the themes that will figure so prominently in the Christological development in the *Church Dogmatics*. The Münster *Ethics* has special interest as Barth's first attempt at a theological ethics which even though it still contains the concept of the orders already adopts a Trinitarian structure, relates all ethics to the divine command, and offers many parallels to the ethics of creation in *Church Dogmatics* III/4. The later chapters indicate Barth's initial thinking about the ethics of reconciliation and redemption, and the whole work opens up fascinating vistas on Barth's approach to various practical issues. Still awaited with anticipation are the volumes of the Göttingen *Urdogmatik* and the important lecture series on Calvin and Zwingli.

An immediate point of interest in the later writings is Barth's more mature thinking on the question of a natural knowledge of God, in which he owed something to intense study of Book I of Calvin's *Institutes*. Barth, of course, never abandons his staunch opposition to natural theology. Among his very last letters are communications with the papacy in which he objects to the Roman Catholic tendency to treat nature and conscience as though they had much the same rank as revelation. Yet *The Christian Life* makes it plain that Barth is not denying that alongside the world's great ignorance of God there is also a knowledge of God that it derives in part from non-Christian sources. Indeed, writing to Carl Zuckmayer, Barth gladly concedes that nature does objectively offer a proof of God, the problem being that we overlook and misunderstand it, as natural science so clearly demonstrates. This clarification enables us to see more clearly the importance of Barth's earlier and later stress on *acknowledgment* as the first essential in the true knowledge of God, which is the knowledge of faith. It also helps us to appreciate more fully Barth's insistence on the rationality of creation in consequence of the rationality of its Creator. Finally, it brings into focus the need for a clearer definition of what Barth specifically means by "natural theology" and why to the very end he maintains his resistance to it.

For the rest, the last letters and the little pieces assembled in *Final Testimonies* proved to be an indispensable part of the Barth experience because of the insight they grant us into Barth's character, into the essential humanity that may so easily be lost in the theology. The letters make particularly good reading from this angle. Consider the humor of Barth, as, for example, he faces the surging flood of Bultmannian teaching. He playfully alludes to the new disease of Bultmannitis, which leaves it victims severely undernourished. He styles the Bultmann school as the company of Korah, compares them to garden gnomes, and thinks the whole movement is like a car with four flat tires (some people prefer to travel that way!). J. A. T. Robinson's *Honest to God* reminds him of the mixed froth of three brews (Bonhoeffer, Bultmann, and Tillich) that people are now peddling and drinking as the latest elixir. As Barth sees it, the best response to this whole theological madness is to treat it with the ridicule it deserves.

Consider, too, Barth's integrity. He has little patience with a student who gets his recommendation for one course of study and then promptly wants to do something else. When a nomadic relative asks how she may serve God, he replies that he cannot help her if she will not learn first the discipline of service in a job. He bluntly tells a theological student who still has ideas of a human building up of God's kingdom that if he persists in this nonsense he should take up any career but that of a pastor. He thinks the silly students who regard themselves as the gravediggers of theology and the explorers of a new ethics should learn what it really is to study instead of engaging in endless discussions of hermeneutics, the speech-event, and demythologizing. He finds little theological substance in the uproar of the student movements of the sixties, his whole sense of academic and spiritual integrity being offended by the way in which a handful of pompous professors and a few hundred excited students and candidates upset the whole process of solid learning and instruction.

Consider, however, the mellowness of the aging Barth. In answer to his lifelong opponent Werner's severe criticism of his *Evangelical Theology*, he not only asks for a little of the reviewer's beloved "reverence for life," but thinks it a pity that two elderly people should part on such terms. Reminded of a public attack on him by a former Safenwil parishioner, he says that he simply laughed, as he did also when a letter in a Zürich paper compared his Christmas radio sermon to the performance of a cabaret artist—a new experience, "but there may be something in it!" Above all we see a new gentleness in Barth's final contacts with Emil Brunner, with whom relations had been so strained since the vehement *No* of the thirties, and to whom, when Brunner was on his deathbed, he sent a last assurance that the time for "No" had long since gone, for all of us live only by the fact that a great and gracious God speaks his gracious "Yes" to us all.

Consider finally the steadfast faith of Barth. From first to last he has confidence in the power of Holy Scripture as God uses it to speak his own Word. This is why he insists on strictly biblical preaching. This is also why he advises his daughter-in-law to let her skeptical father quietly read the Gospels instead of bothering him with the Gnostic theorizings of Teilhard de Chardin. Barth is also bold to bear witness to his faith. Thus in his very first meeting with Zuckmayer he tackles him with almost embarrassing directness: "How about you and religion? Does it mean anything to you?" Above all, he has his faith set firmly on Christ, and it is to Christ that he ultimately gives testimony. This is why at the end of a radio program devoted to his favorite composer Mozart and to various aspects of his own career, he seizes on the word "charismatic" and talks about that other grace where he is really at home. Grace for him is not a concept but a name: Jesus Christ. *He* is that grace, and Barth's whole concern, he says, has been to emphasize this name and to say: "In him." There is no salvation but in this name. In him is grace. In him is the spur to work, warfare, and fellowship. In him is all that he has attempted in life. It is all there in him. Appropriately, then, Barth asks that the program end with Mozart's little *Missa brevis* in D Major and most appropriately with the concluding *Agnus Dei:* "O Lamb of God, that takest away the sins of the world, have mercy upon us, grant us thy peace."

Not everyone can hope to enjoy the Karl Barth experience with the same length and breadth and depth as it has been my own good fortune and high privilege to know. Nor will the experience take the same form for all who by choice or chance may come to undergo it. Some will come with greater openness and sympathy, some perhaps with indifference or skepticism, and some again with antipathy to Barth either as a man or as a theologian. Yet within the measure of what is possible and no matter what may be the initial or the final reaction, here is an experience that all who make a serious pretense of theology and all who have an authentic concern for ministry should not on any account miss. It is not enough merely to read second-hand accounts, so many of which are superficial and incomplete. All genuine students should learn to know a little of the man now that materials are more readily available, and all of them should unquestionably dip into the more exacting theological works, beginning perhaps more easily with the *Evangelical Theology* but not hesitating to take in something of the magisterial *Church Dogmatics.* The aim, of course, is not that any of the readers should become Barthians; Barth even doubted whether he himself might be described as such and he certainly did not want such a fate for others. Nor is it the aim to make Barth the object of sainthood or hero worship; after all, quite early in his public career he learned the significance of the pointing finger of John the Baptist. No, the authentic Karl Barth experience means profiting in some way or another by the life and work and insights of this great Swiss teacher who on any human showing must rank as the greatest of our modern theologians. The profit may come from absorbing the biblical or historical instruction. It may come from wrestling with the deep dogmatic themes, whether in acceptance, modification, or rejection. It may come from following up the practical implications for Christian ministry and conduct. Finally and supremely it may come, and ought to come, from entering into a fuller understanding and appreciation of what is after all the heart of any theology that is worth the name, the revealing and reconciling grace of God the Father, the vicarious life and death and resurrection of God the Son, and the living witness, by Scripture and scriptural proclamation, of God the Holy Spirit.

Learning the Meaning of What I Believe

T. H. L. Parker

Any attempt at autobiography, but especially an autobiography of the mind, will become simple where the reality was complex, ordered where that was confused. Progressions of thought will be presented as deliberate resolutions of problems when they were in fact consciously carried on only by fits and starts, to be left in the intervals to digesting by some other level of consciousness. What will be remembered and shown as a firm and clear conviction was more often a conviction being held more strongly than other, inconsistent convictions. But we shall not get anywhere if we are too Henry Jamesian in our self-analysis. Biography may be deceptive, but it is not impossible for it to show something of the truth.

At any rate, true it is that one day in the earlier part of 1939 I was going to play squash at Ealing and needed a book to read in the tube train. I must have wanted a change from Robert Bridges's *Shorter Poems,* my usual companion, and so looked about for something in my theological college library. The books were kept behind wire mesh—whether to protect them from the students or the students from them I could never decide—and from within the cage a title caught my eye and seemed, if not (in my then idiom) wizard, at least promising a change from the former Poet Laureate. Black print on red cloth proclaimed *The Word of God and the Word of Man.*

If I said that from that day Barth, like *la belle dame sans merci* had me in thrall, it would also be true—in a sense. As a factual description of myself in those far-off years it would be misleading. Robert Bridges continued to fit snugly into my jacket pocket; Westcott, Lightfoot, and Hort were still romantic heroes; Quiller-Couch, undeservedly kind to me at this time, was still my arbiter in literary taste; I still argued passionately for Plato; I was still capable of wearing a black tie on the occasion of the death of W. B. Yeats. There is no need for me to describe my thinking, such as it was; the discerning reader will already have perceived it by the names I have mentioned.

Nevertheless, I had begun to read Barth, not steadily but now and then, and things were being slowly sorted out in my mind. It was not at all that I carried out a root and branch appraisal of my intellectual position in the light of his theology, or even that I attempted to construct a synthesis between Barth and my very ignorant and romantic type of Platonic Christianity (which I had taken to be Bible Christianity). Rather, things began to sort themselves out and Barth's theology began to gain dominance in my mind.

What was it in *The Word of God and the Word of Man* that caught and held me? There was something more than an attraction to the style, so strong and firm, so precise and nervous, speaking clearly, decisively, passionately, memorably. When you have someone who has read his Bible daily from the age of thirteen, who is brought up as a rather old-fashioned but pietistic evangelical Anglican (and therefore believes in the activity of God in his world, in the centrality of Christ and his cross, and who knows that he must "trust and obey") but yet someone who, being a literary sort of youth, has fallen in a big way for those Sirens whose voices so worried better men than himself, like St. Jerome and St. Gregory, someone who, after the pleasures of reading English at Cambridge, is confronted by the less than well-written and usually very arid theological textbooks he has to mug up in order to pass his General Ordination Examination—supposing such a person, is it surprising that *The Word of God and the Word of Man* should seem so wonderful to him? For he said to himself, "This is what I have been reading in the Bible"; and although he did not then say it, he was drawn by a theology that was expressed in strong, clear, masculine language. In contrast to the dreary textbooks, here was exciting theology; in contrast to romantic Platonism, here was a firm and unequivocal statement of the initiative and activity of God.

I have, I see, not once used the word *new* in this account—a fact that genuinely reflects my attitude toward Barth from the first. I had never so far as I know heard the name Barth but once in my life—and even then it made no impression on me. But my feeling on first reading Barth was that, to borrow the opening words of *Arabia Deserta*, "A new voice hailed me of an old friend."

After theological college followed a curacy (for the dreary textbooks had somehow got me through the examinations). I found myself in a smallish town of which I grew very fond but which had the great disadvantage of possessing nothing that could justly be described as a good library. I had therefore to rely on my own books and those of my vicar. He possessed, and lent me, Barth's *Epistle to the Romans.* This I found a heady draught and I fear I must have been one of those babes in theology whom Barth exhorted not to read his *Romans* enthusiastically. I read it enthusiastically, if not infrequently bemusedly, in season and out of season. I read it while on sentry duty in the Air Raid Preventions Headquarters of our town. This martial exercise entailed sitting in a lobby and asking to see visitors' passes—in practice, sitting in a lobby and reading *The Epistle to the Romans.* A man would enter; I would ask to see his pass; he would reply, "It's alright, chum; they know me in there"; and I, grateful that the incident could be resolved without bloodshed, would return to the boundary between time and eternity, the tangent that touches the circle without touching it, the dry canal once filled with living water, the minus sign before the brackets.

During the first two years of my ministry my life was in such a turmoil with trying to learn how to do my work in an extremely busy parish, with coping with pressures of A.R.P. duty (not usually so amusing as I have made out), and with having the joys and responsibilities and problems of being newly married that I really had no time to order my thoughts. All had to be for the moment or, at furthest, for the next Sunday. Through this period of strain and stress *The Epistle to the Romans* accompanied me, perhaps adding to the strain, but certainly providing an intellectual stimulus and forming my mind theologically.

As a part of my "priest's examination" I was required to write a short essay on a subject of my own choosing. Inspired by *The Epistle to the Romans,* I chose to expound St. Paul's argument in Romans 1–8. Absenting myself from felicity awhile, I set out to give my own exposition, altogether apart from Barth. This piece of work received flattering notice from the Bishop's Examining Chaplain, the great B. J. Kidd, so I was encouraged to try the path of theological writing rather than of persevering in poetry and novel-making.

Yet, although it was Barth who brought about this change of direction, I did not feel any urge to make him the subject of my studies. This was partly, perhaps, because he was too personal a matter for me; partly because I thought (and still think) that he was too close in time to be seen clearly and justly (and at that time, of course, he was still very much at work; volume II of the *Kirchliche Dogmatik* had not yet been published); partly, I dare say, because he was just too difficult for me to tackle.

If I did not study and write on Barth, it was he who not only provided the impetus but also directed my course. When I moved to a second curacy in Cambridge, it meant that I had incidentally the run of my own university library. I intended to devote my studies to the English Reformation in general and the Thirty-nine Articles in particular. But I was advised first to get to know the Continental Reformers. So, knowing that Barth frequently praised Calvin, I made a start with that Reformer.

The direction my Calvin studies took may also be ascribed, if perhaps indirectly, to Barth. He had confirmed and assured my belief in the Bible as the authority for thinking and practice. My basis for this belief had previously been the precedent belief that the Bible was written under the inspiration of the Holy Spirit in a way analogous to the Platonic theory of inspiration as expressed in the *Ion* (which I had read in Shelley's translation). When I was at theological college, confronted with what seemed destructive literary criticism of the Old and New Testaments, I sought refuge in books bearing some such reassuring title as *The Bible Is True*. When I had been reading Barth for a while this problem faded away in the light of a different emphasis. While still holding to the doctrine that Holy Scripture is inspired by the Spirit, I left the "how," the method of inspiration, open, looking at the divine origin of Scripture analogously to the Incarnation and to the Holy Communion, and no longer to poetic inspiration à la Plato. This reorientation to Scripture generated a renewed commitment to the message of Scripture in my ministry in study and parish.

Related to this, Barth confirmed and established the concept I had been taught of the preacher's office and duty that he must proclaim the gospel he has learned from Holy Scripture and that therefore sermons ought to be expositions of Scripture. This view Barth both confirmed and also sharpened and made more critical. Was I, were the evangelicals among whom my lot was cast, really preaching the same message as the Bible? Whatever the evangelicals did (and I began to distrust more and more the path they continued to tread), I had no doubt and no hesitations about what *I* ought to try to do in the pulpit.

This renewed commitment to Holy Scripture and to the preaching of the Word of God also swung my studies in a certain direction. After a few months wandering in books, I found that Calvin had not only written many commentaries (several volumes of the Calvin Translation Society edition had their pages still uncut after a hundred years in the university library!) but that he had also been an assiduous preacher, and many of his sermons were in the *Corpus Reformatorum* edition of his works. As I read them I found another Calvin from the Calvin known in England, the author of the *Institutes*, the rigorous disciplinarian of Geneva, the murderer of Servetus. More important, here was a subject dealing with the Bible and also with preaching, a subject that went hand in glove with my own parochial ministry.

As we now go on to consider changes of opinion more precisely, we shall have to begin by emphasizing what has already appeared clearly enough, that Barth's influence on me was the strengthening and readjusting by clarification and demarcation of positions already held rather than a complete change or replacement of opinions. And yet this also is not quite accurate. One may hold all the same beliefs after as before an event, an encounter, a critical period— and yet all will be quite different. The same beliefs rule in the mind, there has been no blinding revelation of "the new," no casting away of things outworn, outgrown, but just—how shall I express it?—just a different slant on the same beliefs. Of course, "a different slant" is really more revolutionary than the harmless idiom sounds. It means that you have shifted your position and therefore see the objects of your belief in a different perspective, in a different light, in different interrelations.

It will be easier to indicate the new position to which Barth led than to try to distinguish differences within the beliefs themselves (even if I could trust my memory for forty years' past ideas). The position is a compound of several elements, all of them obvious enough, even elementary. We need look at only one or two of the most important.

The first element may be described as an awareness of the objectivity of God. This sounds so obvious that I am almost ashamed to write it down. But if one ponders the spiritual tendency of a pietism reinforced with an ill-informed Platonism, one will soon perceive that the objectivity of God, although it is accepted, is not the all-dominant force in that way of life. For a pietist will tend to be so concerned with his own inward and spiritual state that God becomes less and less objective, outside himself, and may even be assumed into his own being. Then God becomes above all a friend, the closest friend of all, and prayer becomes an inward-turning movement. To one in that state the awareness of the objectivity of God is a wonderfully liberating force. To know that God is; to know that God is God;

to know that God is, apart from oneself; this knowledge of itself readjusts all other, not only "sacred doctrines," but all knowledge whatsoever.

The second element is the awareness that God is one with man without ceasing to be other than man. The objectivity of God, the otherness of God, is the necessary truth that rescues one from pietism. But its own tendencies are no less disastrous than pietism itself. Nor can it be maintained in isolation in the light of the Incarnation, which was the Incarnation of God himself, God not other than but one with man. We had been taught at theological college about the difficult problem of the transcendence and immanence of God and had been told to hold them in balance. I have this moment looked up the subject in the books we used on the Thirty-nine Articles and find my memory confirmed. E. H. Bicknell called these two "counter-truths"; for W. H. Griffith Thomas, Christianity "teaches the essential truth of both positions." What a slippery tightrope we poor young theological students were supposed to balance on!

But from Barth I learned (gradually, no doubt) the central truth of all truths, that the objectivity of God, the otherness of God, the Sovereignty that he will not give to another, is not to be separated from his becoming one with man, from his becoming the one who serves men and even puts himself at their disposal. These are not two contradictions or even two countertruths to be held in balance, but as Christ is one, the sovereign Lord who is the Servant, the Servant who is the sovereign Lord, so these are one. It is not an *either-or,* not even a *both-and,* but it is *simul . . . et simul.* In being the one he is at the same time the other.

The second element, then, is the truth that the sovereign Lord God became one with all men without ceasing to be the sovereign Lord God. If this is grasped in its strict meaning, pietism and Platonism will not long survive. For revelation is not the earthly point of a hierarchical chain (even if this is viewed as Father—Son—the flesh of Christ by which we ascend to the knowledge of the Son and thence to the knowledge of the Father); rather, it is the presence, the "visitation," of the Lord God himself. How then shall a man who is thus encountered by God take possession of the revelation or meet the revealed in any other spirit than that of deepest abasement and humility? The mystery of revelation is that in giving himself in lovingkindness to man God does not give up or lose his sovereignty.

God's self-revelation is a matter of condescension, of grace, and correspondingly, from man's side, of amazement. "Grace," I read in

Barth's *Romans,* "is the incomprehensible fact that God is well pleased with man." Into the word *incomprehensible* Barth is concentrating the Pauline and Reformation doctrine of justification by faith alone. If the biblical witness to the holiness of God and the unrighteousness of man is true, it is impossible that God should be well pleased with any man. That he is so can be ascribed only to his loving mercy, his grace. From man's side it is utterly incomprehensible. Should it be the slightest degree comprehensible (that is, if a man can see grounds in himself why God should be well pleased with him), then it is not grace. But since God's grace is incomprehensible, man's reaction can only be one of amazement—in the words of Psalm 126, inscribed in the chapel of Bethel-bei-Bielefeld: "When the Lord turned again the captivity of Zion, then were we like unto them that dream." We thought we were still asleep, we could not believe our ears. The incomprehensibility of grace gives the deathblow to pietism, which, like any religiosity, will take it for granted that the Lord is and will be a good friend and so will be free to treat him with familiarity. Vanished is the mystery and with it the amazement conceived of grace.

The space allotted to me has been filled and I must stop. Writing this, calling up the ghosts from the winding caverns of memory, and pondering upon the meaning of it all, I have seen the essential truth of my presentation more and more clearly. When I have insisted that, at least in my earlier acquaintance with his writings, Barth taught me nothing new, it has not been intended ungraciously or orgulously. What he did—what I was not capable of doing for myself—was service sufficiently revolutionary. It was to teach me the meaning of what I believed.

How to Be Most Grateful to Karl Barth Without Remaining a Barthian

Dietrich Ritschl

Has he actually changed my mind or have I merely changed my mind on him? This double question occurred to me when the editor of this volume asked me for what he called an "honest appraisal of whether Barth has actually changed your mind." Both questions, of course, must be answered in the affirmative.

My personal encounters with Karl Barth occurred at two very different stages in my life. When I was young—too young at nineteen—I was his student and tended to look at the world through his eyes. I am not sure whether I liked him then. I admired him and—at times—was afraid of him and of his judgment. And then, many years later, came my second encounter. I was a more or less Americanized theology professor. He was old, very old. I was no longer afraid of him and did not look at the world and at theology through his eyes. It was then, perhaps, that I began to love him. He came to our house (where we spent the summers and sabbaticals). I drove him through the country, he told us stories, he made one of our boys eat two or three full meals at a restaurant and enjoyed his immodesty. He read my books and was surprisingly mild in his judgment. I visited him in the hospital and he wanted me to read to him from the newspaper, once even from Goethe.

These, of course, were two stages in rather sharp contrast. But let me go step-by-step in attempting to retrace the changes in my mind.

I

My boyhood dream was to become a physicist and to enter into the relation between physics and philosophy. My decision to abandon physics after four semesters and to take up the study of philosophy and theology, however, was prompted by my experience of the Christian student community at Tübingen and by my reading of Schleiermacher's *Speeches* and all the works of Albert Schweitzer I was able to obtain. Karl Barth was outside my direct vision. I merely had heard of him and, of course, of Bonhoeffer. When my sister married Bonhoeffer's nephew, I recall lecturing to my brother-in-law, also a student of physics, that Barth's and Bonhoeffer's theology might have been very useful in the church's struggle against Nazism but that I would hope Schleiermacher and A. Schweitzer would shape the future of theology (today, when assessing the papers of our young students, I sometimes think of these embarrassingly premature judgments).

II

The professors in Basel, famous as they were, were not the best lecturers in the world. W. Eichrodt and O. Cullmann read their notes, as did W. Baumgartner without ever looking at us. Karl Jaspers, whom I admired, was impersonal and ultimately disinterested in communication (about which he unfolded so many wonderful thoughts). Heinrich Barth, the philosopher and Karl Barth's brother, was very severe and did not radiate overly much joy. Only Fritz Buri was a lively teacher—but I was on my way to other theological camps. Karl Barth's lectures were didactically and rhetorically not brilliant, but they were convincing. He, too, was unable to communicate with a large group of students without having his manuscript at hand. I recall one day when he thought he had left his notes at home and when he sent Lollo (Charlotte von Kirschbaum) to fetch them, he stood helpless behind the lectern for twenty minutes without opening a discussion with his audience. When Lollo returned without his notes and when he found them in his pocket, he saved the situation with a good joke and started lecturing. And his lectures were real lectures! The students were able to witness the dynamics of newly created thoughts. His cooperation with Lollo in producing the text for the lectures, revising them in the light of spontaneous comments during the lecture, thereby completing the on-going text of the *Church Dogmatics,* a team-work following a disciplined time schedule—that was a truly phenomenal and noticeable experience. I think it was this creativity and originality that convinced me of Barth's theology. As I write this sentence, I begin to wonder whether it was really this and not so much the content of what he said. But in all honesty, I think what struck me was above all this creativity. And his seminars! I remember a seminar on Schleiermacher. Having myself conducted a seminar on Schleiermacher's *Kurze Darstellung* with a large group of very able students in Heidelberg this summer, I think with all the more admiration of the way Barth led that seminar. He wanted us to listen to Schleiermacher and forbade us any critical utterances until the last one or two sessions. His method in conducting seminars was authoritarian, to be sure, but it allowed and required a maximum of interpretative power on the part of the students.

III

Barth's teaching helped me to come to grips with the other parts of a theological student's responsibility. Exegesis and history found their place. Practical theology—E. Thurneysen was our teacher—was placed high on the list. I can still hear Barth say, "Why do you want to become anything other than a parish minister?" He was not interested in creating professors or ministers for a "special ministry." His thought enabled me—better, it persuaded us—to label other theological authors, to assess anything and anyone. I began to read him. The impression became stronger: here is the tool, here is the yardstick for measuring any voice and any thought on theology. I began to develop some skeptical thoughts, but they were held within limits. I was surprised that Barth did not respect my philosophical studies. He had contemptible things to say about Jaspers (with whom I was writing my dissertation). Instead, he recommended to me his brother Heinrich. I did not fully believe that he really meant that. I somehow felt that he might have been right on Jaspers but I was irritated at his ultimate lack of interest in other academic disciplines. Although he always affirmed his great respect for this or that discipline, for medicine and for the natural sciences, for anthropology and for philosophy, I began to feel that the results of all of these fields of research literally meant nothing to him, nothing to his theological inquiry. I still believe this today, although I hear the voices of his defenders ringing in my ears. I would never deny, of course, the immense knowledge Barth had in these fields, especially in German philosophy.

IV

While working as an assistant minister in Switzerland for two years and for six years as a minister to German-speaking people scattered all over Scotland, I began to encounter the Barthians. First there was a comradeship among us, later a certain reservation on my part. They seemed to know all the answers. The rural Swiss and the Scottish forms of Barthianism are not quite the same. But they are sufficiently similar to increase the doubts of a young theologian as to whether or not Barth's theology is the only way in which to look at the Bible, the church, the world, and one's fellow human beings. My theological dissertation was in Patristics—assessed by such different scholars as T. F. Torrance and Henry Chadwick—and it was my new love for the early Fathers that showed me a greater breadth of theology than Reformation theology was able to encompass.

With this heritage and these doubts I came to the faculty of Austin Seminary, where I had five very happy years in the field of New Testament and Patristics. During this time I also served as minister of a little country church outside the city. I wanted to learn something about the nonacademic climate of American Christianity. I read more of Barth during these years and deepened my friendship with his son Markus, who would later be my colleague on the faculty of Pittsburgh Seminary. I also became acquainted with analytical philosophy. I think I must have been intellectually intolerant during these years. In fact, I was uncertain where to go theologically. But I was all the more convinced—and still am—that I am more interested in people than in books and—ultimately—more concerned for the church than for the academic truth of theology. Although such thoughts may horrify my Barthian friends, I would maintain that, in the last analysis, I learned them from Barth himself and that the aging Barth has given me some signals of endorsement.

V

There was, however, an ambiguity in his tolerance. During my years at Pittsburgh we would continue spending our summers at home in Switzerland. Not a summer went by without several visits to Barth. I reported to him on new books and thoughts in the States, on developments in Eastern Europe, on the Prague Peace Conference (when it was still possible to be part of it) and on my own projects and plans. His reaction to new concepts was ambiguous. At times he seemed unwilling to accept any kind of theological work that was more than a mere continuation-in-detail of his own dogmatics, at other occasions he demonstrated a surprising degree of tolerance in appreciating different and new approaches. I have never quite understood the reasons for this ambiguity. One summer he asked me to bring Eberhard Bethge along in order to have him explain what Bonhoeffer really had intended with his charge of "revelation-positivism." Bethge was more than tactful and polite; he was leaning over backward to clarify his friend's criticism. But Barth absolutely refused to listen.

VI

During these years as well as after Barth's death, when I was at Union Seminary in New York and then back on the Continent, Barth's way of criticizing his enemies began to irritate me substantially. It was then that I consciously changed my mind and set out to do non-polemical theology. I was and still am tired of polemical theology. It seems to me that it has had its time and that Barth's theology represents a climax but also the end of a development. I do not mean to say that we should not fight for certain positions or insights. But we should be cognizant of the fact that our own perspective of theological truth is relative to other perspectives. Moreover, it seems to me that my generation began to realize that we as Christians are in a minority situation and that we no longer live in a Christian world. Although we may have learned this from Barth, I doubt that he ever realized it himself. Not only did he never learn to love the Orthodox or Anglican liturgy, he did not travel to Eastern Europe (except for the trip to Hungary), not to speak of the Third World. His theology was done entirely within the categories of Continental Protestantism and Catholicism. To put it more strongly: I think that Barth never in his life had an in-depth conversation with a truly nonreligious communist, an atheist, a Muslim, or a Hindu. So what? my Barthian friends may ask. Have we, who have had all of these experiences, produced a more constructive and helpful theological system? We have not, of course, and yet we have found something he had not seen. We have discovered that personal confidence surpasses intellectual-theological agreement; we begin to see the integrating function of theology in relation to the human and social sciences; we are beginning to learn how to relativize our words without losing insights. At times it occurs to me that I had heard Barth say something along those lines toward the end of his life: the freedom to do theology in entirely different ways. Perhaps it is true that if we today make use of this freedom, we owe the insight into it to Karl Barth.

VII

I hope I was right in saying that we today know how to "relativize our words," having gone through the cleansing fire of analytical philosophy. We have done perhaps no more than the first few steps. I for one would say that Barth's work has prompted me to search in this direction. I do not think I would have gone into Wittgenstein as well as into modern philosophy of science had it not been for a deep dissatisfaction with the linguistic imprisonment in which I find entangled those Barthians who go about their work today using Karl Barth's language of yesterday. I observe that quite a number of the colleagues of my generation seem to have felt a similar impulse. Not only are we today unafraid of words and terms that horrified Barth, we do not suspect to find the truth resting within words either; that is, we trust that the same insight can be expressed in many different ways. Moreover, although we know that a convincing conclusion must be won by deduction and not by induction, we shy away from deducing theological insights from statements fabricated by theological reflection. There is no doubt that Barth has done just that; the implications he draws from his doctrine of the Trinity or from his concept of revelation are but two examples. This does not turn the theology we want to do into "inductive theology," least of all does it imply that we want to abandon a primarily biblically oriented theology, or that we want to produce a non-Trinitarian doctrine of God. On the contrary, we want to stick to all of these basic programs, though using language with greater care (and freedom), avoiding the identification of affirmations with theological results or truths. In using the plural form "we," I mean to indicate my firm conviction that theology today should be done by teams or groups of scholars. In one of the last conversations I had with Karl Barth, I told him that my ambition was to be a good player in the orchestra of theologians. He quite strongly disagreed and smilingly admonished me to play a solo instrument. I think now, as I did then, that the time for this is over.

VIII

Having recently published a "Systematic Theology" myself, it is time to ask the question whether I—or one of my friends and colleagues—should aim at constructing a new system of theology. I would emphatically deny this. While Barth always claimed not to have created a system, he surely was the architect of a gigantic theological system. Regardless of whether we come from Barth or from Tillich or from one of the great Roman Catholic or Orthodox teachers ours is not the task to copy them by coming up with an additional system, criticizing or replacing the old ones. Our theological and ecumenical situation today is entirely different. A former period has come to an end, new tasks lie ahead of us. Let me spell this out more concretely for those who have listened to Barth: We will not only *say* that Israel is important for Christian theology, we will have to *do* theology with the Jews. Our task is not merely to *stress* the *importance* of ecumenical work, but to actually *do* this work. Nor will we *merely respect* the various sciences in the university, such as medicine, anthropology, philosophy, and law, for we will have to *engage* in interdisciplinary discourse, attempting not to teach the truth but to seek it and to make a meaningful Christian contribution to such discourse. And, although it was courageous and magnificent that the Barmen Declaration stated that there are no areas of life where Jesus Christ is not our Lord, ours is the task to *fill in positively* what it means to be a Christian in this or in that situation, in these various areas of life. We will *not only state* what God's grace in Jesus Christ means for humans—for "man," as Barth and his contemporaries said—we will have to *spell out in detail* and test the theological assertions with reference to men and women, children and old people, the healthy and the sick. The concrete human existence must not get lost; economic, sociological, and psychological, even psycho-linguistic insights belong right in theology. What Barth rightly attempted with regard to politics in his qualified rejection of a two-realm doctrine must also be applied to all of these areas of inquiry. Such theological work will not result in a new system.

IX

Why, then, my early change from Schleiermacher to Barth? To be sure, I was not conscious of what had happened to me at that time. Now I begin to see that Western theology—which will surely no longer hold its monopoly—both in Protestant and in Catholic terms, will have to focus on these two great Christian teachers, Schleiermacher and Barth. The intra-Christian and intra-Western polarity in theology is no longer Origen *vs.* Augustine, much less is it Luther *vs.* Calvin, nor is it, it seems to me, the ultimate choice between Thomas and the Reformers. Rather, it is the bi-polarity of Schleiermacher—

Barth. I do not think that we should take our stance in the school of only one of them, nor should we compromise between them. New theological work is called for. This was driven home to me for the first time in very clear terms when I edited Barth's lectures on Schleiermacher given in the winter of 1923-24 (this volume 11 in the Karl Barth *Gesamtausgabe* has also appeared in ET as *The Theology of Schleiermacher* [Grand Rapids: Eerdmans, 1982]). Here you become the witness of a head-on collision! But don't be mistaken: Barth did not change his mind on Schleiermacher in his later years, despite the claim of some of his followers. This book shows the strength as well as the dangers of the two theologians. While it may have been wise to choose between the two of them in the middle third of our century, it would be foolish to do so today.

X

Grateful to Karl Barth? I am immensely grateful to him for having liberated Continental European theological thought from improper questions and false dilemmas; for having rehabilitated the Reformers and many of the early Fathers to become partners in the discourse of systematic, not merely of historical, theology; for having created an entirely new epistemology with regard to the "things of God," based on the clear priority of reality over possibility (an epistemology not without problems); for having involved Roman Catholic theologians in theological discourse; for having attempted to incorporate ethics into dogmatics; for his convincing emphasis on the central importance of the doctrine of the Trinity. Although I have reservations about the term *dogmatics,* I am grateful he called his work *Church Dogmatics.* I am grateful that he shared with Schleiermacher the zeal for the church and that he taught us to see theology as a function of it.

Good News from Karl Barth

Robert McAfee Brown

When I was in seminary, during World War II, the works of the "continental theologians" were hard to get. Emil Brunner was the one to whom most of us looked when we gazed across the water, and there were a few things of Barth's around—a group of challenging essays entitled *The Word of God and the Word of Man,* a forbidding first "half-volume" called *The Doctrine of the Word of God,* and the sprawling *Epistle to the Romans.* The essays were unsettling, we didn't quite know how to cope with "half-volumes," and *Romans* seemed very "one-sided" (a favorite term for disposing of Barth in those days). Here was somebody, we gathered, who rejected reason, philosophy, and any kind of human effort and espoused a quietistic "vertical" relationship to a God who offered his revelatory presence quite capriciously even within the Christian dispensation.

It took a long time to get over such caricatures after the war, but the struggle was worth it, even though I don't rest as comfortably within the Barthian universe as I once did. My own initial appreciation of Barth was immensely accelerated when I was doing graduate work (1948-49) and was looking for a dissertation topic. Daniel Jenkins, a British friend spending a year at Union Seminary on a Commonwealth Fellowship, suggested that I look into a British Congregationalist, P. T. Forsyth (1848–1921), a man whose name, at that stage of my theological innocence, was a brand new one. Forsyth's books were also hard to come by, though he was enjoying a renaissance in Britain and his books were beginning to be reprinted.

I do not know who first described Forsyth as "a Barthian before Barth," but the study of Forsyth, interesting on its own terms, prepared me for a more affirmative *entré* into the world of Barth. Forsyth had an intense "Christological concentration," a powerful biblical orientation emancipated from literalism, a never-yielding emphasis on the priority of revelation over reason, and a view of grace that distinguished it in the sharpest possible terms from the realm of nature (so much for Thomism). His favorite contrast was between the Word and the world. Starting with the Word, he felt, we could embrace the world, but the reverse wouldn't work; there was no way to get from the world to the Word. We were dependent on the divine initiative and any response on our part was the result of grace.

Walking in such a theological landscape, one might expect to feel very much at home when encountering Karl Barth, and as T. & T. Clark began to produce the huge black volumes of the *Church Dogmatics* in the post-war years, Barth more and more dominated the landscape. Conditioned by my Union mentor, Reinhold Niebuhr, to be wary of Barth's theology in the light of its genteel treatment of post-war communism, I was surprised by and surprisingly supportive of the famous letter Barth wrote to an East German pastor, Johannes Hamel, in which Barth gave advice on how to live a churchly life in Germany's East Zone. I wrote an introduction to the English translation of this letter (Barth–Hamel, *How to Serve God in a Marxist Land*), one of the few places where I felt on the opposite side of the fence from Niebuhr. In the late 1950s, John Bennett and I team-taught courses on Barth at Union Seminary, during the exciting time when every six months or so a new slice of revelation would arrive from T. & T. Clark in the latest "part-volume," as the Scottish publisher tried to catch up with all the German volumes that had appeared during the war. A major portion of my sabbatical, 1959-60, was devoted to reading accumulated volumes of the *Dogmatics*, an endeavor that persuaded me that Barth could write faster than I could read! My translation of Georges Casalis's *Portrait of Karl Barth* brought me into even closer touch with Barth's life and thought.

During these years, without calling myself a "Barthian" (though the term was sometimes applied to me by those who meant it pejoratively), I felt some obligation to present Barth on his own terms, free of the stereotypes he seemed destined to live under in the eyes of most Americans. So I gave a lot of attention to him in the classroom, on the lecture circuit, and in a few articles. A move from seminary to university teaching raised the ante: could Barth communicate to undergraduates? I used his small book *The Humanity of God* for several years and in those heady days when undergraduates were responding to Barth, Tillich, Niebuhr, Buber, Bonhoeffer, and Bultmann, he did ring a few bells. Perhaps it was the life story—the attraction to socialism, the costly objection to Nazism, the refusal to apply to communism the same strictures he had applied to National

Socialism—that made Barth seem alive, and made an examination of his theology seem interesting and even important. For whatever reasons, alive he remained.

As we moved through the civil rights struggle and then into the Vietnam War on the very volatile Stanford campus, the direct impact of Barth on me receded, but I know with assurance that during those years it was the story of the German "church struggle," the rise of the Confessing Church, the clarion call of the Barmen Declaration, and the political engagement of people like Barth and Bonhoeffer that nourished me. The 1960s called for a clear "No" to the government of my country, just as the 1930s had called for a clear "No" in Germany, both based on a clear "Yes" to the God of the Bible—and since that now seems to me the Christian recipe for the 1980s, whatever legacy I have from Barth is still very important to me.

Let me now try to identify less biographically and more systematically some of the items in that legacy.

1. One of them has already been implied—Barth's unwillingness to separate theology and ethics. In a context of academic speculation, when areas in the theological curriculum were compartmentalized, Barth refused to say, in effect, "I'm now creating a new theological system, and when it's done someone else can draw the 'ethical implications' from it." Instead, he incorporated his ethics into his dogmatics, insisting that they must be interwoven, establishing a constant dialogue between the two, and providing no possible way for theologians to deny that the ethical dimension was part and parcel of the theological dimension. No one, he made clear, can flee from the demands of the world into the refuge of the sovereignty of God, or use grace as an escape from works, or allow gospel to preempt concern for law. That contribution of Barth's will abide, no matter what the fate of this or that portion of his massive system may be.

2. Barth's approach to Scripture is also enduring. In those early years of Barth's impact in North America, once the stereotypes began to fall, American theological conservatives and quasi fundamentalists found Barth especially threatening. With his dependence on Scripture he sounded like one of them, but was really the most dangerous of all, because he wasn't, in fact, one of them. I especially appreciated Barth's insistence that just as we can be guilty of docetism in our treatment of Jesus Christ (falling into the trap of claiming

that he only "seemed" to be fully human), so, too, we can perpetuate a scriptural docetism (suggesting that the Scriptures only "seem" to be fully human documents, when they are in reality protected from any human error). To Barth, part of the glory of Scripture is that its truth stands out in the midst of the time-bound nature of the documents, shining through all the human errors and smudges, just as the glory of Jesus Christ stands out in the midst of the time-bound nature of his first-century existence, with all of the limitations that placed on his perceptions. In other words, Barth is the theologian of incarnation rather than theophany, insisting that the revelation comes *through* the contingent, rather than bypasses it. So, too, with Scripture; we can hear it more truly to the degree that we do not have to be reassured with infallible guarantees. More important than whether or not the serpent in the Garden spoke Hebrew, Barth wrote early in his career, is the question of *what* the serpent said, and with that content we must constantly wrestle.

3. To speak of Scripture is already, as has been apparent, to speak of Christ; it is Christ who is the Word of God, rather than the book that tells us about him. No Christian theology worthy of the name can be other than Christocentric, and whatever else Barth's theology is, it is Christocentric. God did something, Barth constantly reminds us, in a narrow strip of history on a narrow strip of land, in Palestine, and we are forever bound to respond to the nature and the content of that action. If the "early Barth" stressed the theme of Koheleth that "God is in heaven and you are on earth," the mature Barth sings praises to the God who is also on earth as well.

We will never exhaust the meaning of that event, nor will we ever fully understand it. Theology can be no more than ongoing reflection on the fact that no matter how great the distance between God and ourselves seems to be, that distance has been overcome, not by our effort, but by the divine initiative, for which we can only give thanks.

4. This kind of Christological centrality saves theology from being pretentious. It can be no more than a fragmentary attempt to reflect on a subject never fully compassable. For Barth, it seems to me, theology is no more and no less than an act of gratitude, an attempt to say "thank you" to God with the life of the mind, by reflecting, for the purpose of sharing through proclamation, what the meaning of God's gift to us really is. Gratitude (*eucharistia*) follows grace (*charis*), Barth once remarked, as thunder follows lightning.

It may, however, seem like stretching the point to describe Barth's theology as a "fragmentary attempt," considering those huge "part-volumes," but there are at least two rejoinders to the charge. The first is that it *was* a fragment, in the sense that it was never finished; Barth died before the system had reached completion. And the second rejoinder is that he died content that it was so. Nothing would have been more foreign to Barth's approach than for him finally to lay down his pen and say, "There now! I have finally captured the Word of God with human words." It was not only appropriate, but important, that the *Church Dogmatics* remain incomplete. Had he "finished," in the sense of having completed a human system, Barth would surely have been the first to acknowledge that what he had done for his day would have to be begun all over again for the next day. A Reformed theologian does not write for posterity but for the moment.

5. An important part of Barth's legacy to me was his reclaiming of the doctrine of election. As a Presbyterian, expected to take election, predestination, providence, and other related topics with deep seriousness, I long found myself in a doctrinal corner, fighting defensively for what seemed a lost cause. It was *CD* II/2 that emancipated me. It was liberating to read Barth's comment that when he approached this topic he had expected to follow his master Calvin, and then discovered that in faithfulness to Scripture he had to break with Calvin, and declare that the doctrine of election was not a doctrine of impenetrable darkness but of indescribable light, God's ultimate "Yes" to humankind. The Scriptures, Barth affirmed, proclaim God's unconditional choice *for* us rather than against us, the preeminence and prevenience of God's grace, the God who has already chosen us before the foundation of the earth.

We can, of course, deny that truth about ourselves and live as though it were not so—in which case, Barth says, we live a lie—but we cannot make God's "Yes" into a "No," we cannot reverse the decision on our behalf that God has already made. What we *can* do is live in the light of that blazing truth as grateful recipients of a gift we could never have earned or even anticipated had it not already been there for us to appropriate. For Barth, we do not start from sin and discover our "need" for grace; we start with the reality of grace, in the light of which we can see for the first time how deep was the "need" from which we have already been delivered, if only we will believe that it is so.

Now whatever else that is, it is definitely "good news" as opposed to bad news. And as I reflect on the baleful influence on the church and on the human *psyche* of centuries of Augustinian-Thomistic-Calvinistic predestination, I am grateful that the shroud has been lifted by Barth and that the human endeavor can again be affirmed as an endeavor blessed, rather than cursed, by God.

In the last fifteen years, my theological and personal concerns have shifted from the continent of Europe to the continent of Latin America. Having once tried to assure that Karl Barth got a fair press in the United States, I am now concerned to assure that liberation theology gets a fair press in the United States. (This is a more difficult task, I have found, since more people have a stake in discrediting liberation theology than ever had a stake in discrediting Karl Barth. Presidents and State Departments never worried overmuch about Barthian theology; they worry a great deal about liberation theology, which is a great compliment to liberation theology.) Many of my friends see this new concern as a repudiation of the earlier concern. How, they ask, can you resolve the difference in approach between Karl Barth and, say, Gustavo Gutiérrez? On the face of it, the distinctions do seem sharp. Whereas Barth insists on starting with a commitment to revelation rather than to politics, Gutiérrez starts with a commitment to the victims of political injustice, so that theology becomes, in his well-known phrase, the "*second* act." Barth must surely be turning in his grave.

But despite the apparent methodological impasse, there are some mutually reinforcing convictions. For one thing, neither position starts *de novo*. Barth was a political being in his daily life, a Swiss pastor who was also a socialist, before he read the Epistle to the Romans in a new light—and he has always brought those convictions to his examination of Holy Scripture. Gutiérrez, on the other hand, in his full definition of theology as the "second act," calls it "critical reflection on praxis *the light of the Word of God.*" If Barth brings an implicit praxis to his examination of Scripture, Gutiérrez brings an implicit biblical orientation to his examination of praxis. Which comes first is a kind of chicken-and-egg conundrum; what is important is that *praxis and the Word of God continually interact* for both Barth and Gutiérrez. Moreover, as Barth struggles with the biblical message, the content of the message he hears is remarkably similar to the message liberation theologians hear. As Barth puts it, in words that might just as easily be found in Gutiérrez: "God always takes His stand unconditionally and passionately on this side and on this side alone: Against the lofty and on behalf of the lowly, against those who already enjoy right and privilege and on behalf of those who are denied it and deprived of it" (*CD* II/1, 386).

And it was Dietrich Bonhoeffer, Barth's friend and ally, who wrote eloquently about the need for his bourgeois friends and himself to discover "the view from below," to see the world from the perspective of the disadvantaged—an almost exact counterpart to liberation theology's emphasis on seeing the world from "the underside of history."

The fact that liberation theology, like Barth's theology, is so biblically rooted, is an important point of convergence between the two. The above quotation from the *Dogmatics* could be duplicated dozens of times over in other volumes by Barth as he reflects on the God of the Bible. Indeed, we could go on to argue that it is this same biblical rootedness that gave Barth the courage to issue a clear "No" to Hitler, and likewise gives Latin American Christians the courage to say "No" in their own situations of tyranny.

Barth may write a great deal more about who God is "in Himself" than liberation theologians, but when he writes about God in relation to the world, he and liberation theologians are surely close to one another—both proclaiming a God who is involved in the world, who sides unconditionally with the victims for the sake of all, who proclaims and enacts justice, and in whose worship the concerns of the "very least" are never lost but are seen with a new kind of importance, so that just as God acts on their behalf, all of God's children are empowered to do the same.

There is one area of Barth's thought, I must confess, that has never spoken to me, and that is the extraordinary attention he gives to angels. I seem to have enough trouble thinking about God and the world without extending my purview to the heavenly messengers. Even so, and adopting the angelic idiom for the moment, I am almost persuaded by Barth's assurance that when the angels play music before God, they play Bach, but when they are just playing *en famille,* for their own enjoyment, they play Mozart. And I allow Barth the right to decide that when he gets to heaven, the first person he will seek out is not Calvin or Schleiermacher, but Wolfgang Amadeus Mozart.

But I still have this problem. When all the claims have been made, when all the scores have been compared, when all the recordings have been listened to, it is still my considered judgment that the angels play Beethoven *both* before God and among themselves and that if I ever make it to the celestial realm, the one *I* want to meet is Ludwig van Beethoven, his hearing restored, his 42nd symphony just completed.

Barth

Martin E. Marty

Barth for the Student

In the late 1940s when I entered theological school, American students were coming to terms as never before with European theology written by their contemporaries or near seniors. In the nineteenth century there were ties, of course, but America generally went its own way. In the first half of the twentieth century American liberalisms were also largely home grown. Before the war the Niebuhr brothers, the immigrant exile Paul Tillich, and translators or promoters of note like Walter Marshall Horton and Wilhelm Pauck had agitated for more attention to "crisis" thought. Yet even the humanistic crises accompanying the Great Depression were not profound enough to make European theology of the post–World War I vintage a necessity.

World War II changed that. While it was still a "foreign war," our slightly older classmates had seen something of the terror and futility that Tillich and Karl Barth and others had known at first hand in World War I. They brought with them a new set of inquiries about human nature and divine purpose. At the same time in secular thought various existentialisms held sway. Those of us a bit too young to have seen military action but too close to those who did were busy, with them, piecing together or retrieving theological visions that might inform personal life, scholarly quests, and, most of all, the ministry to which we aspired.

At such a moment and for the decade that followed, Karl Barth was preeminent. He had his best chance to affect America and Americans stood the best chance of understanding what he was about. As a Lutheran at a conservative seminary, I was much warned about how Barth mixed law and gospel—the primal Reformed intellectual sin, we were told—and that he was shaky in respect to seventeenth-century-style Lutheran scholastic views of the Bible. Yet it was clear that those who warned us were deferential, if not filled with awe, when they spoke of Barth. That added to the lure. While many of us struggled with the German or waited for translations, we were awe-filled as we saw our seminary seniors lugging around those status symbols, the heavy white-linen, black-imprinted volumes of the *Dogmatik*. In due course, we learned to crack them, if not to carry them.

Barth never "took," all the way, for most of us. We were experiencing a more congenial neo-Lutheran analogue to his Reformed dialecticism. For us, Karl Holl and Anders Nygren and a host of German and Swedish historians and system-builders were more helpful. Yet it was clear that Barth was the one by whom we measured. He was the eponym, the "name-giver" to an age, and if he had, one day, to yield to Paul Tillich, at mid-century he spoke to us.

How did he speak? He taught us, through the scope and authorial voice, the very volume and the burden of documentation, to take the Christian life of the mind seriously. Let some interpreters see him as antihumanistic, belittling human effort; his own achievement contradicted this. What an astonishing humanistic achievement it was for him thus to have saturated himself with textual understandings until they became part of his nature. What an effort his work was: so magnificent that it seemed effortless. All this could be stunning to a student: who dared picture writing a dogmatic or systematic work without his equipment? Yet he actually did inspire us by suggesting to an academic and ecclesiastical world that such efforts were not irrelevant. What was more germane to us than this attempt to speak about the Word of God in the shattered world? His remained the paradigm of theological work.

Barth for the Minister

In the early 1950s, when my class and its cohorts ahead and behind entered the ministry, the American Christian mood was anything but naturally inclined to Barth's message. Though it was only a third of a century ago, this moment for ministry seems almost beyond mental grasp today. The G.I.'s were home, eager to sink in roots. They and their spouses were breeding large families, deserting farms and old urban ghettos for suburbs. Europeans and Africans have been on this continent for 49 decades; religiously, it seemed, the 1950s was the only decade when "everything worked." The affluent society had been born. We liberals debated how, justly, to slice the pie that seemed always to be growing. There was McCarthyism and there was Cold War; the racial issue was looming and the economy had a soft underside. The Korean War presaged an era of futility in international affairs. Yet these marked our ministries less than did the expansive, prosperous mood.

When one looks back on the artifacts of that era in religion, it is hard to see how Barth could ever have gotten a hearing. Catholicism was in a triumphalist mood. Bishop Fulton J. Sheen was effecting conversions and the converts helped build showy marbled convents and seminaries, many of them now deserted. Sunday schools boomed. The mainline Protestants were at the cultural center. Evangelicalism was showing a new face. "Positive Thinking" and "Peace of Soul" were best-selling spiritual options. W. H. Auden spoke of *The Age of Anxiety,* fashionably for intellectuals, yet who internalized this theologically?

Barth continued to haunt the postwar preachers, however. In a nation that was tempted to collapse the ways of God into the ways of Eisenhower, to identify divine purpose with our righteous "crusade against atheistic communism" and for "the American Way of Life," Barth was at least a corrective. There was no danger that his critical theology could prevail. It was not of our soil, did not speak our tongue, seemed too remote and stern and even gloomy for the suburbanites to whom we preached. Those who did other kinds of venturesome ministry, for example in the model of "racial integration" in the urban slum, reached elsewhere for messages of hope. Barth was concerned with ethics, but he did not seem to address our issues.

If the American congregations never quite caught the spirit of Crisis Theology, the dialectic, the Theology of the Word, or, perish the word, "neo-orthodoxy," I still believe that they profited from their ministers' encounter with Barth. If we were so given to immanentalism and progressive and positive thinking *with* his impinging presence—he seemed to be scowling over our shoulders from some point behind the pulpit when we accommodated too much—shudder to think of what we would have been without that impingement? God was not that convenient American invention, to be consulted and taken captive the way one uses a watch in a pocket or leads around a puppy. God was, despite our turns and twists, beyond our turning and twisting, Wholly Other. God's thoughts were not our thoughts. Whatever we did take captive by definition could not be God.

I did not believe then and do not believe now that Karl Barth made a contribution to the centrist mode in theology and preaching. It was not that we would take a dab of him and then a dab of American liberalism, and live halfway between. Pascal said somewhere that one should take into account the extremes of thought, but not stake out a position halfway between. I would say of him what in a corollary I would say about someone like Jacques Ellul. It is not that he is "half right about the whole Christian faith." Instead, he is "wholly right about half the Christian faith." Only when he began to write *Christ and Adam* or *The Humanity of God* did he come close to talking about that other half: in an immanental, incarnational, condescending, identifying God. As a historian who had few tools for speaking about God, I was one who was led back to biblical God-centeredness and away from the temptations of Christomonism by Barth more than any other. The people to whom I ministered profited by the refractions of his grand vision through the preaching and teaching of the saints I half-helped half-equip in those years.

Barth for the Professor

In the middle of the course of my years, precisely at age 35, I for the first time walked into the classroom and began to teach "The History of Modern Christianity." The preoccupation of the class was with America, but not in isolation from Atlantic culture. This meant that the shadow of the European giants remained strong, even if it was not the focus of the teaching.

Where this teaching occurred created some problems for any interest in Barth. The University of Chicago Divinity School cherished terms and concepts he did not: pragmatism, empiricism, liberalism, and the like. While the only time I met him was on the Chicago campus—his son Markus was teaching there during his triumphal American visit—and while he packed Rockefeller Memorial Chapel for days, the theologians there made quite a point of being "non-neo-orthodox." Joseph Haroutunian gave Barth an occasional try in the classroom, but got little hearing. We historians did not have to be captive of current ideology or ethos; Barth already belonged to "the church fathers," as historian Jaroslav Pelikan reminded us. Yet inevitably we worked in an atmosphere not then conducive to Barth studies.

Still, he haunted and influenced. I might buy into the then fashionable critique by Dietrich Bonhoeffer that Barth's was a "positive of revelation." With others, I did buy into the enduring suggestion of Paul Tillich that Barth's was a system devoted to *kerygma*, but at the university theologians needed to do more with *apologia*. At *The*

Christian Century we agreed more with Reinhold Niebuhr than with Karl Barth in their postwar and Cold War political debates. I find that few of the categories of the sort that become instinctive in one's thought derive from Barth in my case. Tillich's ontology may have been further from my comprehension than Barth's antiphilosophy, yet Tillich's predicates and categories (like "catholic substance" and "Protestant principle") or Bonhoeffer's (like "world come of age") were more adhesive.

Despite all these qualifications, these damnings with faint praise, these elusive references to a haunting more than an informing presence, I have to say that the encounter with Barth has been lifelong and has been salutary. It is time to say why.

First, Barth forces a fresh engagement with biblical texts. More than anything else, he has been *the* commentator on Romans for people like me. He taught us more about hermeneutics than the hermeneuticians would let us conclude. Like Origen and Luther, he was more the "diviner" than the scientific critic of Scriptures. Watching him in action, reading his sermons to Basel prisoners, studying the biblical citations, going with the drift of his biblical thinking when he did not cite it—all these have stood us in good stead when we want to transcend the moment and stand on the horizon of the text.

Second, while Barth did not set out to be a historian and probably never provided a true rationale for historical curiosity on the Christian landscape, he shows that the Bible is in a tradition and that tradition is in the Bible. His array of Patristic, Medieval, Reformation, and modern citations informed and set an example.

To these two I would add a third: his ecclesial posture. Barth does provide a meeting point for liberals when they retrieve tradition and evangelicals and Catholics when they want to be expansive. This is important for junctures and coalescences that transcend existing patterns.

What remains above all, however, is the confidence he gave us that we must, and perhaps can, speak of and about and to God. Language analysts, symbolic logicians, phenomenologists, and most other schooled philosophers can point to all the problems in reference when God-language comes about. (Curiously, these philosophical critics have a symbiotic relation with Barthian theologians: it was puzzling and remains interesting to think how many secular or radical or even "death of God" theologians almost easily phased out of

Barthian God-talk to non–God-talk. And, sometimes, phased back again. But that is a topic for another day.)

We knew, we know, the problems of God-talk, yet speak we must if anything like Christian faith and witness and theology are to continue. Saul Bellow once said, "Being a prophet is nice work if you can get it, but sooner or later you have to talk about God." It has been my experience that in the contexts of agnostics, secular-minded pluralists, and those suspicious of the claims of faith, it is expected that this be sooner, not later. Ancillary theological themes can be postponed, made part of trivia quizzes. Theme Number One, theos+logos, God-thought, God-language, most efficiently and focally comes up first. Barth certainly is not the only model when this agenda comes up, and he may not even be the best. But no twentieth-century serious thinker more consistently pressed it to the front of thought, writing, and preaching than did he. For that, he will live as fashions come and go.

Relevant Remembering

Elizabeth Achtemeier

During the years 1952-54, my husband and I—both graduate students at Union Theological Seminary in New York—were given fellowships by that institution for study abroad. Our first year was spent at Heidelberg University, Germany, our second at Basel University, Switzerland, under the tutelage of Karl Barth. It was an unforgettable experience that certainly played a part in shaping the foundations of the theology that has served me all my life. While I would never lay claim to being a "Barthian"—a term that Barth himself abhorred—and while I would not say that Barth has particularly changed my thought, he certainly exercised an influence on it.

Strangely, it was the personality of the man that made perhaps the strongest impression on me. Barth was, and remains, the most important theologian of the twentieth century—the Luther of our age—the giant who is given to the church only once in every hundred years or so. And yet, in his relations with his students, there was no one more humble and unassuming than Karl Barth. A rumpled, lovable, old giant of learning, Barth acted toward us as a pastor. He inquired with genuine interest about our living arrangements, about our adjustments to living abroad, about our thoughts and youthful views. When my husband spent an hour and a half talking to Barth in the latter's study, Barth thanked my husband for the time spent with him! Indeed, he took special interest in the American students studying with him and at the end of his seminar with us accompanied us all to the local Weinstube for conversation into the night. (My husband still has a volume of the *Dogmatics* with a pencil sketch of Barth's plan for the peace of Europe, drawn that night on its cover.)

I mention these things because it seems to me that part of the test of any theological system is the evidence of the working of that theology in the life of its author. Does that which is being propounded bear the scriptural fruit of the Spirit in the life of the propounder? Some of the leading theologians of the twentieth century fail that test, but Karl Barth did not. The faith he taught produced in him love, joy, peace, kindness, gentleness, self-control. He lived by what he believed and the life he lived, he lived to Christ. Perhaps that personal witness has meant more to me than anything else.

Second, I think I learned during our year with Karl Barth what it really means to be a member of the Reformed branch of Christendom. My husband and I attended Union Seminary in New York at a time when it was perhaps one of the leading seminaries in the world. Reinhold Niebuhr (the other giant of our century), Paul Tillich, John T. MacNeil, Cyril Richardson, James Muilenburg, and Paul Scherer peopled its faculty. They taught us daily of the Word of God. And yet, when one listened to Karl Barth's lectures, American theology by contrast seemed awash in subjectivity. Barth held out to us the Word in itself, in all its power, all its authority, all its transforming effectiveness. The Word of God in Jesus Christ—there was the Rock of the church—and that Word and the Reformed emphasis on it took on for me a sustaining, clean, and power-laden objectivity I had never encountered before.

In his formal lectures, Barth simply read to us the manuscript of the *Kirchliche Dogmatik*—inserting, I might add, commas and corrections in the manuscript as he read. We in this country, with our concern for "communication" and effective teaching techniques, would consider that a poor instructional method. But the Word, proclaimed in those lectures, needed no help from teaching techniques. It came through loud and clear, working its way with us—converting us, judging us, inspiring us. The lectures, read from a manuscript, had the effect of proclamation, and Barth's classroom often, for me at least, became not a lecture hall but a church.

Barth's dedication to the sole authority and power of the Word of God was illustrated for us in three minor incidents at the time. First of all, while we were in Basel, Barth was engaged in a dispute over the stained glass windows in the Basel Münster. The windows had been removed during World War II for fear they would be destroyed by bombs, and Barth was resisting the attempt to restore them to the church. His contention was that the church did not need the portrayals of the gospel story given by stained glass windows. The gospel came to the church only through the Word proclaimed. As a homiletician, I think I prefer to say that the church needs to appeal to all the senses, not just the hearing of its congregations. Nevertheless, the incident was typical of Barth's sole dedication to the Word.

Second, after our return to this country from Basel, Barth and Reinhold Niebuhr confronted one another at the Assembly of the

World Council of Churches that dealt with the theme "Jesus Christ, the Hope of the World." No two men were more alike and yet no two men were more different. Barth, in his dedication to the Word of God, wanted to talk about eschatology. Niebuhr, whose theology dealt primarily with a Christian doctrine of man, thought such eschatological emphasis was irrelevant. We are indebted to both great thinkers, of course, but once again the incident is illustrative of Barth's sole dependence on the Word of Scripture. That which stood in the Scripture could not be irrelevant for him. The dimensions of that Word determined for him the breadth and depth of his thought.

Third, after Barth's visit to this country, I recall with what shock a professor at Union Seminary reported a conversation some had had with Barth. Someone had asked "the Baseler lion" what he would say if he met Adolf Hitler. Barth's reply was "Jesus Christ died for your sins." How irrelevant, how simplistic, how utterly absurd seemed that reply to American pragmatic ears! And yet I suspect Barth's answer was his way of saying to his listeners, in the context of a brief conversation, that finally the church has only one message—Jesus Christ and him crucified.

Perhaps nothing in Karl Barth's theology has been more important for me, however, than his emphasis on the otherness of God and on the uniqueness of the Word of God over against the wisdom of the world. That God is God and not man, that he is Creator and not creature, that his ways are not our ways and his thoughts are not our thoughts, and that we are totally dependent on the revelation given through the Word of God—those central elements of Barth's thought have been confirmed time and time again for me in a lifetime of study of the Scriptures.

No one who understands the Old Testament, it seems to me, can ever find the revelation of the God of the Bible to be mediated through the structures of the creation. On its very first page, through the centuries of priestly theology reflected in Genesis 1, the Old Testament carefully delineates God's relation to his creation. He does not emanate out of the chaos, as do the gods of those Mesopotamian cultures whose mythological language is borrowed by Genesis 1 and then promptly demythologized. God is not contained in any way in the processes of nature that he creates. His uniqueness over against human beings, who are given his image, is carefully guarded. Rather, the God of Genesis 1 stands over and above his creation as its sovereign Lord and his only relation to his creation is through his

Word—a thought that is then reiterated in the opening chapter of the Gospel according to John.

Confirming such a testimony to the absolute otherness of God, then, are all the law and the prophets. The second commandment of the Decalogue forbids us to find in anything in heaven above, or in the earth beneath, or in the waters under the earth, any medium of the revelation of God. And Deuteronomy argues, throughout its sermons, that God is one—unidentifiable with some diffuse *numina* permeating all, unlike any fertility god or goddess of the sown land, and known only through the voice of revelation given at Mount Horeb. To that the prophets add that God is indeed holy God, that is, totally unlike anything or anyone in all creation. "I am God and not man, the Holy One in the midst of you." And so Israel's reliance on the weapons of Egypt is reliance on flesh and not spirit, according to Isaiah, and the plans of human beings are futile over against the plan of almighty God. Indeed, according to Second Isaiah, the heavens may vanish like smoke and the world wear out like a garment, but God's salvation of his own is forever and his deliverance will never be ended.

That such a God, then, in order to give us such eternal salvation, has revealed himself fully in his Word made flesh, Jesus Christ, obviously must become the center of all human thought about him, and there is no other place or person to whom we are to look for the revelation of the God of the Bible. God has made himself known through his Word—through his speech and action that have found their final reinterpretation and incarnation in Jesus Christ. Our knowledge of God and our experience of him are totally dependent on that Word.

Barth's insistence on the Word as the sole medium of revelation is, I believe, fully consonant with what we find in the canon. And to say that that insistence has been important for our time is putting it mildly. It was just such an insistence that preserved the true nature of the German Confessional Churches that proclaimed, in the Barmen Declaration of 1934, that the only source of the church's proclamation is "Jesus Christ . . . the one Word of God," and acknowledged that the church knows no other "events and powers, figures and truths" as sources of God's revelation.

That that Word of God is totally inaccessible within human wisdom and the structures of creation is, moreover, of crucial importance to the theological debates of our time. Such an understanding of God's revelation stands over against all natural and process theology that would think to comprehend God within the structures of the created world. It calls into question the identification of God with the "Ground of Being," à la Tillich and J. A. T. Robinson. And it challenges any theological formulation in which the qualitative difference between Creator and creation has been blurred or overlooked.

Similarly, Barth's insistence on the uniqueness of the Word of God, unknown to human wisdom—which is fully consonant with Paul's understanding of that Word, in 1 Corinthians—challenges every identification of that Word with the ideologies of our time or any supplementation of the Word by those ideologies. Human wisdom cannot add to the Word of God—whether that wisdom be Marxist ideology used to supplement a liberation theology, or feminist ideology used to supplement the biblical understanding of the equality of female and male in Jesus Christ, or modern medicine and psychology used to counter the scriptural judgments leveled against homosexuality. The confession of faith that lay behind the Barmen Declaration is fully as applicable to the modern theological struggles of the church as it was to Nazism in its day: "Jesus Christ, as he is attested for us in Holy Scripture, is the one Word of God which we have to hear and which we have to trust and obey in life and in death." Through that Word, and him alone, we are given the way to the Father and the truth of him and his life. Through that Word, and him alone, we are given our salvation.

Three Confidences

James A. Wharton

The pilgrimage to Basel in the 1950s was an easy one for Presbyterians from the American South—perhaps too easy. There was every chance that we would find in Karl Barth nothing more than an impressive European champion for the most cherished elements of our native theological traditions. We had already been taught that serious theology begins with the absolute sovereignty of God, not only in the ordering of the universe but most significantly in the matter of our salvation. God was never to be conceived as the human written with a capital "H." The distance between the two was absolute and qualitative.

We thought we already knew that Jesus Christ was God's decisive gift of self to and for the world, and that the doctrine of the Trinity grounded the Good News of Christ in the being of God.

We had been catechized to accept the Scriptures of the Old and New Testaments as the Word of God, "the only infallible rule of faith and practice." Yet we had been spared the worst abuses of fundamentalism. It was congenial to conceive the Word of God as the Living Word, to be listened for among the unmistakably human words of Scripture. It was in just this unmistakably human form that the words of Scripture conveyed to us all things essential for what we are to believe and what we are to do. That Scripture is able to do this "infallibly" is testimony to the faithfulness of God and the power of the Holy Spirit, rather than to some intrinsic holiness that resides in the words themselves. It was therefore unnecessary to wage urgent battles over the six days of creation, or the authorship of the Book of Daniel, or the culturally conditioned New Testament advice that women should keep silent in church.

We had also been schooled to pay high respect to Reformed confessions of faith (in our case the somewhat iconic and for that matter none too "Reformed" documents of Westminster). And one carried the bias that the *Institutes* and the commentaries and the sermons of Calvin were truer to the gospel than many more recent excursions into theology and exegesis.

113

We did not have our Bad Boll, but there were elements of evangelical pietism in our tradition that made us ready to hear that "Jesus ist Sieger!" And we were not altogether shocked to discover the exalted role Karl Barth assigned to prayer both in the work of theology and in the daily existence of the church.

As Southern Presbyterians we may have inherited an against-the-stream mindset born of a lost cause, and the (largely imaginary) oppression of a Yankee intellectual imperialism. Barth's militant, embattled stance over against prevailing intellectual fashions, Nazi tyranny, pre–Vatican II Catholicism, and any theological or political opposition may have struck century-old chords within us.

Moreover, we were heirs of an ecclesiastical polity that added a distinctly political dimension to faith, made capital "C" Church a grand word and set the Church over against the world in a quixotic way. What kind of a dogmatics could there be except a *Church* dogmatics? In short, all the receptors were there to transform Karl Barth into a *Kirchenvater* for Southern Presbyterians, alongside R. L. Dabney and Stonewall Jackson. Had our pilgrimage to Basel, in the 1950s, simply taken us back home?

Unease with our own tradition in the 1950s made us wonder whether Karl Barth was indeed saying what we had always believed, in impressive new ways. Where had the bold, against-the-stream theological protest been, among Southern Presbyterians, in the days of Senator Joseph McCarthy and the Korean War? As viewed from Basel, the Supreme Court decision of 1954, the clear beginnings of the civil rights movement, and the subsequent failure of Presbyterian reunion on the grounds of white Southern racial and political and cultural views exposed our tradition as a bastion of the Southern status quo. If we held so many of Barth's cardinal theological themes in common, why had we not discovered there the resources Barth found to withstand the tyranny of cultural fashions and political oppression?

Three decades after my first pilgrimage to Basel, these and other questions are still there. Whatever else Karl Barth may have done for me, he has not preempted the answer to any serious theological question. He has not afforded us a system that can be manipulated to produce theological rightthink. I take very seriously the admonition he always gave us that the *Church Dogmatics* were never to be repeated by rote. His work was occasional, limited to a time and a place and a set of temporal urgencies. The whole work of theology is to be done all over again, in new times and new places, responsive to a new set of urgencies. There are those who doubt that he ever genuinely gave us permission to disagree with him. He would not have been Karl Barth if he had ever stopped contending, in his militant way, for that right theology that was surely to be found at one place or another in his work. But I prefer to think, on the grounds of his own theological analysis of the human situation, that his advice was seriously intended, theologically if not always emotionally.

It is that analysis, particularly with respect to the curious work of doing theology, for which I am most permanently grateful. It is permanently useful to hold open the possibility that we may be human beings and not gods. The finalities we lust after, whether in religion or politics or economics or personal life or in society at large, all lie in the province of the gods. If we conceive ourselves as gods, we will not only continue to lust after the finalities, we will do our best to create and master them. If we conceive ourselves as human beings, we are free to regard the finalities we lust after as idols, "no-things," false gods. We are at liberty, in the absence of finalities we can hope to create and master, to accept the limits of our humanity, to "glorify God and to enjoy Him forever." Something like this view of things is distinctively set forth in the biblical story. I suspect it was this perspective, more than any other aspect, that Barth discovered in the "strange new world of the Bible."

Barth undertook to demonstrate that it is altogether possible, in this modern and postmodern world, to think the world outward from the center of God's gift of self to the world in Jesus Christ. All the resources are there in the biblical story to conceive human life as it is with breathtaking realism. Nothing we human beings do or can contemplate doing is altogether shocking once we have thoroughly absorbed this biblical realism about the human condition. We do exist in a condition of brokenness, and our lust for the finalities is tragically flawed.

But no significant longing in human life, if it is both loving and just, is without substance if Christ is Lord and the future belongs to the Lord and Giver of life. It is that realistic optimism about God that Barth meant to convey to the world. And he understood himself, in that enterprise, to be standing in the succession of an unbroken chain of witnesses, stretching back through the Reformers and the Fathers (and mothers!) of the Christian tradition to the time of Christ.

Whether this is optimistic realism or realistic optimism, it provides a rare perspective on the character and meaning of human life. Since it is grounded in God who alone is Lord, who alone is both loving and just, this perspective forbids us to take ourselves or any-thing else in the created order with absolute seriousness. Since it finds the being as well as the intention of God toward the world made flesh in Jesus Christ, the Living Word, this perspective commands us to place the love of God, concretely expressed in love for people, higher than any other good. We are forbidden to flee any of the realities of this world, as if the truly human could be realized in some other dimension besides just this space, and just this time, under just these circumstances. We are commanded to translate whatever we think we know about God into specific attitudes and actions that reflect, in just this broken context, the love and the justice and the righteous-ness and the faithfulness and the peace and the truth of God, which are God's gift of self to us in Jesus Christ. We are forbidden to despair, because Christ is Lord, because through Christ's life, death, and resurrection God's victory for our humanity is sure. We are commanded to hope because our incompleteness and our broken-ness are shared at unutterable depth by Jesus Christ, and the promise of Christ's resurrection is that we shall be made whole. The last word about the whole tragic and glorious human experiment is that "in Christ, God was reconciling the *kosmos* to himself, not counting their trespasses against them" and that nothing "in all creation has any power to separate us from the love of God which is in Christ Jesus our Lord."

I have learned from Karl Barth that this is indeed a rare and distinctive perspective on the meaning and character of human life, one not to be met with in our common human wisdom about how things are, nor in the general run of religious and philosophical speculation. And I have learned that it is a waste of time, and in any case disobedient, for Christians to try to package what we have to say to ensure the widest possible acceptance of our point of view. The question is truly not whether we shall take the world by ideological storm, but whether we shall be obedient to the faith that has been delivered to us, whether we shall give to the world some sign that we are prepared to love as Christ has loved us, whether we shall under-take to reflect God's love, God's justice, God's righteousness, God's peace, and God's truth in the world. The self-acceptance to which the gospel of Christ invites us by all means includes our fragmentariness. We do not possess all truth. God alone does. Cross and resurrection leave us without any conceivable grounds for self-righteousness, for arrogance, or for the ambition to dominate culture by imposing our perspective upon others.

Once that has been said, however, the church of Jesus Christ does have a God-given responsibility to clarify its own perspective on the character and meaning of human existence, not toward the end of ideological domination but toward the end of faithfulness.

I have learned from Karl Barth that we do not require the permission of any external authority, of any prevailing mindset, or of any "objective" or "neutral" forum of opinion to get on with that work of clarification. The most interesting thing we Christians have to offer the world is still the rare and curious thing we have to say about God. And the only authentic way to get at that is still by means of attentive and faithful listening to Scripture, insofar as possible on the Scripture's own terms. Still we need to test what the church has said, and is saying, by its norm, which is Scripture. Still we need to listen for the Word within the words, relying on the internal testimony of the Holy Spirit. If the church is thereby aided toward significant discipleship in a pluralistic world, then it will have rendered its best service to that world.

It seems to me that this authentically modest thrust of Barth's work is more easily perceived now than it was during his own lifetime. Massive ideological shifts and conflicts swept Europe from 1917 to 1968 with an intensity perhaps unparalleled during any comparable time-span. There is no doubt that Barth's work was caught up in and dramatized by those shifts and conflicts. Barth's combative, uncompromising style served to make his voice heard far beyond churchly circles. He was perceived, not without justification, as an ideologue (or perhaps a counter-ideologue) battling against heavy opposition for the conscience of Europe. Modest is not the first adjective that comes to mind when describing Barth's style or his titanic theological output under those conditions.

The most clearly obsolescent aspect of Barth's work probably lies here, in its ideological or counter-ideological ponderousness, not only of style but also of approach and sometimes of theological content. He is constantly fighting battles that no longer need to be fought, as it seems now. The ideological struggles that once captivated the best minds and the liveliest imaginations have now paled away into confusion and a large indifference. Power confrontations persist, on a grander scale than ever, but the accompanying rhetoric grows increasingly shrill and splintered and intellectually barren. The prospect is not promising that an ideological breakthrough in the battle for human allegiances can shape the near course of history or avert the underlying terror.

Under these conditions, the church is thrust back upon the modest role of salt and leaven and light. That was its only possible role during the first two centuries or so of its existence. When one looks here and there for the times when the church has served most faithfully and most transparently its own gospel, throughout the centuries, has it not always been in the role of salt and leaven and light? Conversely, the genuinely tragic times in the history of the church have been times when whole cultures were brought to heel by "Christian" majorities, and the church's point was made by cultural and political and not seldom by military power.

I find enduring resources in the work of Karl Barth for this redefined and authentically modest service of the church to the world in the way of Christ. One looks away from the obsolete ideological struggles that dictated Barth's militant and uncompromising style. One translates apparent dead-certainties into fresh questions that may indeed be tested by renewed listening to the biblical story under altered circumstances. One places fresh exegesis in fresh conversation with the succession of Christian witnesses throughout the centuries and throughout the world today, including voices that Barth either never heard or that he chose to ignore. All of this one undertakes as a process of listening for the Word within the words. And none of it is done in the interest of constructing a dominating ideology. All of it is done in the interest of helping the church render a faithful account to the world, through its word and its service, of what it claims to know of God.

Salt must be salt. Leaven must be leaven. Light must be light. The impulse of Barth seems enduringly correct, as I see it, that the church can never hope to discover its authentic character and function by conforming its unique and curious word about God to schemes of thought derived from other sources. It is surely true that the mind of every generation is formed by thought patterns drawn from its cultural and intellectual milieu. But one has a choice. One may set out to conform the church's unique and curious word about God to those thought patterns, or one may set out to discover how the church's word about God tends to criticize and call in question prevailing thought patterns, insofar as they claim to disclose news about who God is, or who we are vis à vis God, or what on earth God is up to, or what God expects of us, or what we may expect of God. Karl Barth tells us that the choice between these two options is decisive, and he charges us to choose the second option if we are interested in clarifying what the church of Jesus Christ is to believe and to do. I continue to believe he is right on both counts.

Finally, one of the most enduring insights I have gained from Karl Barth is his concept of the church. As I put his picture of the church together from many isolated references, we have all the evidence we need for the total bankruptcy of the church as a human institution. The record of the church offers no grounds at all to believe that we have proven religiously wiser, or more courageous, or morally better, or less corrupt than any other collection of people on earth. The words of Paul (quoted from Jeremiah!) apply decisively to the church: "Let those who boast, boast of the Lord!" Every attempt to ground the rightness of the church in the superiority of the historic life-style of Christians is fundamentally flawed, on theological grounds, right from the start. Christianity cannot be regarded as a superior religion because Christians turn out to be superior people. To contend that we are superior, on those grounds, constitutes a denial of the gospel. It issues in the prayer "Thank you, Lord, that I am not as other people." It blocks out the just prayer "God, be merciful to me, a sinner." It arrogates to ourselves the glory that belongs solely to Christ. But, I hear Barth saying, the glory that belongs solely to Christ is, by the grace of God, manifested to the world through the strange, flawed, bankrupt testimony of the church. Not because we are a superior community. Not because we have attained the glory of the resurrection. But because we have been graced, in and through our sinful human existence, to bear witness to the one "whom God made our wisdom, our righteousness, and sanctification and redemption." Concretely, this has meant to me that one can reach out and embrace the funny, sinful old church, just as it is: little old ladies, little old men, little children, warts and all. To do so *is* to embrace the body of Christ. Not because they are so glorious—they really are not—but because Christ has loved them all the way to the end, just as they are. Because Christ has raised them up to bear witness to God's victory and God's truth. Because they embody in all their fragile and flawed and broken humanity the world for which Christ died and for whose sake Christ rose again from the dead. Because the good hope they have been privileged to share is God's hope for all those other sinful and suffering human beings out there. For that reason, and for that reason only, they are privileged to carry the word of God's grace to every nation, as full equals to any man or to any woman or to any child alive; as D. T. Niles put it, as "one beggar telling another beggar where he found bread."

A corollary of this view of the church is that meaning, in any significant human sense, must not only be accessible to our finest minds, but to our simplest hearts. The wonder of the church is that the simplest person who is able to stammer "Jesus loves me" has already broken through to the greatest depth Christians may hope to attain. The varying gifts of the Spirit enable some members of the body of Christ to excel in knowledge of Scripture and in disciplined thought about church and world and theology. But, like all gifts of the Spirit, they are to be expended on behalf of the whole body. Those who possess such gifts are neither elevated in importance above the others nor have they arrived nearer than others to the Way, the Truth, and the Life. The mystery that fascinates Christians is not that we have drawn near to the truth of God in Jesus Christ, but that in Jesus Christ the truth of God has drawn near to us, breaking through the barriers of our sinfulness and our obstinate ignorance.

Barth's intention was that the *Church Dogmatics* might prove useful to those responsible for articulating the gospel in the community of faith. For that work one needs confidence that it really is possible, in our own times, to think the world outward from the center of God's gift of self to the world in Jesus Christ. One needs confidence that God the Spirit is able, in the reading, speaking, and hearing of the Word of God, to quicken hearts to faith, minds to truth, and wills to faithful discipleship. And one needs confidence that the truth of the gospel is so inherently simple and transparent that everything that *must* be said *can* be said in terms a child can understand. Barth's work provides a resource unique in this century for those in serious quest of these three confidences.

Helps from Karl Barth

Bernard Ramm

My encounter with Karl Barth came in two phases. The first was the literary phase, in which I commenced reading systematically the *Church Dogmatics* and other shorter books and journal articles. The second was my personal encounter with Barth when I spent the academic year of 1957-58 in Basel. I listened to Barth lecture. I attended faithfully his famous English language seminars. Every time I could I visited his home at the posted visiting hour (Saturday, 2:00–3:00 P.M.). On those occasions I came with a list of questions and took notes on Barth's replies. These literary and personal encounters with Karl Barth did materially change some of the ways I thought about theology, lectured on theology, and wrote theological books.

The first material change stemmed from a passing remark Barth made to one of his questioners, that if we truly believed that we had the truth of God in Holy Scripture we should be fearless in opening any door or any window in the pursuit of our theological craft. The truth of God can never be intimidated. If perfect love drives out fear, then the belief that we have the truth of God in Holy Scripture should drive out of our minds all intellectual fears about our theology.

I had become a Christian in the last years of the fierce fundamentalist-modernist confrontations. This controversy had the tendency to make an evangelical Christian very defensive, suspicious, and protective about his or her theology. I did fear open doors and open windows. It was a great temptation to live one's theological life within the confines of a small fort with very high walls.

There are occasions when the human mind works with the speed of a computer. In such a flashing moment a whole new strategy for my theological work came to birth. I saw in rapid succession on the parade ground in my mind the futility and intellectual bankruptcy of my former strategy and the wonderful freeing strategy of Barth's theological method. I could be just as free a person in theology as I would be if I were an experimental scientist. With the full persuasion of the truth of God in Holy Scripture I could fearlessly read, study, and listen to all options and opinions in theology.

As a young Christian I had been warned to read only "safe" books, for if one read other kinds of theological literature one ran the high risk of catching the disease. That gift of freedom in theological work has been a mainstay in my own theological work as I have attempted to read as widely as possible in the field of theological literature—and I might add in science and philosophy, too.

The second material impact of Barth's theology upon my own thinking and methodology was from Barth's great respect for historical theology. It has been said that if Barth had turned to the history of dogma instead of dogmatics proper he would have surpassed the great Adolph von Harnack. Even so, the *Church Dogmatics* is an excellent resource for historical materials.

In my early Christian years I was much influenced by a movement I have dubbed American Pietism. It is not so much a specific organization as it is a kind of theological attitude one finds in many places. One of the premises of my friends in this movement was that a Christian could learn all the theology he or she needed by a patient and systematic reading of Holy Scripture and by ignoring academic theology. It was a settled conviction of these Pietists that academic theologians did not teach systematic theology but systematic confusion. I was informed that a Christian reading his or her Bible with an open mind and a dependence upon the Holy Spirit could learn all the theology necessary for the living of the Christian life. Of course these Pietists did have some theological heroes, such as St. Augustine, Luther, Calvin, Wesley, Jonathan Edwards, and L. S. Chafer.

When I started reading *Church Dogmatics* (I/1, which was the only volume translated at the time) I was astounded at Barth's ranging all over the territory of historical theology, and his doing so in the original Greek or Latin text. Here was a theologian who did not believe in "the tyranny of time," namely, that the old is wrong simply because it is old and the new is true simply because it is new. With Barth it is to the contrary. It was possible that a great church father knew his theology better than the neologians of the Enlightenment.

I then began to realize that my pietistic friends were interpreting theology as an exclusive personal subject matter. Barth understood theology as church theology and not the registering of personal opinions (even though a good theologian cannot avoid the latter). One of Barth's objections to the modern ecumenical movement was that so many in the movement understand ecumenicity to be a dialogue among living theologians of different theological traditions. Barth understood ecumenicity as a dialogue not only with one's contemporaries but with the theologians who have gone before. The function of historical theology is precisely to carry on a theological dialogue with the theologians of other epochs. It was this kind of dialoging that saved theology from being merely a registering of personal opinions or from being overly impressed by the current batch of theologians. Some of Barth's most unrestrained caustic remarks were aimed at John A. T. Robinson's *Honest to God* because Robinson was overimpressed by current theological fads. The study of historical theology helps the theologian to write church theology and not merely register personal opinions on various Christian doctrines.

I had some preparation for this, having received my doctorate in philosophy from the School of Philosophy of the University of Southern California. At that time the current faculty in philosophy believed the most basic study in the field to be the history of philosophy. This was based on the assumption that a person could not properly assess or understand with any depth current philosophy and its problems. Accordingly, all candidates for the doctorate in philosophy had to choose the history of philosophy as one of the areas of their doctoral examination. It was not too difficult for me to see that the kind of reasoning that gave the history of philosophy such a prime status also applied to theology. Part of competence in theology depends on learning much historical theology (in fact, Edwin Lewis made the history of philosophy the basic course in his lectures as the best possible background for theological education).

This appreciation of historical theology gained through reading the *Church Dogmatics* greatly molded the way I taught theology. I discussed no topic without a minimum summary of its historical dimensions—and this applied to elective courses as well as courses in systematic theology.

The third way in which Barth changed my thinking in theological methodology was the manner in which he correlated the critical study of Scripture with the inspiration and authority of Scripture. The science of biblical introduction that was introduced into theological studies at the time of the Enlightenment created a fundamental problem that troubles theological education and the church to this day. It raised the question of how the theologian can study Holy Scripture in its human and historical settings and at the same time recognize it as possessing divine authority. The problem also can be posed in terms of the divinity and humanity of Holy Scripture.

From the Enlightenment until now many suggestions have been

made to correlate the critical and theological study of Holy Scripture—too many to enumerate here. But at one end of the spectrum are those who believe that the critical study of Scripture has shown it to be a purely human product possessing no religious authority but to be aligned with the other great religious writings of the human race. At the other end of the spectrum are the fundamentalists, whose strong belief in the authority of Scripture denies the practice of critical studies. Between the two extremes are many moderating attempts.

Barth admitted that his first year of study in a theological faculty gave him a permanent bias against the critical study of Holy Scripture. This was at the University of Bern where his father was a professor. The courses on the Old and New Testaments were not expository courses in which the riches of the biblical truth were explored. To the contrary, the lectures were dry performances given completely over to the critical problems suggested by the text. After one year at Bern, Barth transferred to the University of Berlin and other German universities. When he became a professor he could not maintain an aloof attitude toward critical studies of Scripture but had to forge his own theory.

For my own thinking, I have found Barth's method of correlating the human and the divine in Scripture, or the critical study of Scripture along with the theological exposition of the text, to be the best option among the many that have been suggested (among which there is much overlap). His solution to the problem raised by the Enlightenment with respect to Holy Scripture, its criticism, and its theological relevance, is very fruitful and helpful, especially at two points.

First, he showed me that there is not a one-to-one correlation between the Word of God as it originates in the mind of God and the expression of that Word in the Old and New Testaments. The Word of God comes to us in three different languages—Hebrew, Aramaic, and Greek—and is to some measure refracted because no human language can mirror perfectly the mind of God or his Word. Furthermore, the Word of God came to people in very specific cultures, and just as the Word of God is diffracted as it is cast into different languages it is also diffracted by the culture of the inspired author of the text. Anthropologists tell us that tribe, language, and culture inseparably blend into each other. This *diastasis* or *interval* allows for the linguistic and cultural phenomena of the text and still maintains the theological status of the text as the Word of God. The presuppositions of both fundamentalists and liberals made it impossible for either of them to come up with a new, workable synthesis.

His second help for my own theological reflection was Barth's affirmation that the way a portion of Holy Scripture came to be written or composed does not invalidate it as the Word of God. Whether it was the final product of one author or of an editorial process, each book was accepted into the canon as the Word of God. To repeat, neither fundamentalists nor liberals had any presuppositions in their mode of theological reflection that allowed them to come to this conclusion.

Even with Barth's indifference to much of biblical criticism (because such criticism would never grant to a human book the status of the Word of God), he is not home free. There are some hard problems to face to make his theory workable. But in my opinion his is the best attempt in modern times. His theory does give us a foothold. And we hope that in the future someone will put Barth's thesis together in a more convincing way and we shall know better how to correlate biblical criticism, divine revelation, divine inspiration, divine authority of Scripture, and its place as the Word of God in the church.

Karl Barth: Appreciation and Reservations

Donald G. Bloesch

Besides Luther and Calvin, I count Karl Barth among my principal theological mentors. At the Chicago Theological Seminary and the University of Chicago Divinity School, where I obtained my ministerial and doctoral degrees respectively, I found Barth's theology to be a viable alternative to the neonaturalism of Wieman, Meland, Daniel Williams, and others, which dominated the scene at that time. Conservative evangelicalism, it seemed to me, had capitulated to the modern temper by tacitly accepting an empirical reductionism and therefore failed to provide the solid answers to process thought for which I was looking.

What I appreciate the most about Barth is his strong affirmation of the freedom and sovereignty of God. From this perspective, God cannot be manipulated or cajoled by the priests of the church, nor can his grace be confined to the rites of the church. He is free to speak his Word in his own way and time, and he may or may not use outward or visible means. When God does make use of human instrumentality, it must be seen as being in the service of grace rather than grace being limited to it.

Of course, these themes are also to be found in Calvin, but where Barth differs is that his emphasis is on God's sovereign love rather than his sovereign majesty and holiness. Without denying this other side of the divine being, Barth insists that love is the essence of God and that God's judgment as well as his grace are rooted in God's steadfast love for his creation.

Fully consonant with this emphasis on divine love is Barth's reinterpretation of predestination as the universal election of humankind to redemption. Instead of a decree of reprobation that is intended for the wicked of the world, Barth contends that Jesus Christ is both the elected one and the reprobate. God in Christ has taken upon himself our reprobation, and therefore we are free to be the elect people of

God. Although this election goes out to all, not all respond to it, not all alter their lives accordingly. Barth has made it possible for the church to preach predestination, judgment, and hell in the context of God's unfathomable love without minimizing the seriousness of the state of unbelief.

Barth has also given us an insightful restatement of the doctrine of the atonement without succumbing to the liberal temptation of viewing Christ as a paradigm of virtue rather than a mediator and sinbearer. For him, the cross of Christ signifies not a sacrifice offered from the side of humanity that procures divine forgiveness (as in Anselm) but the manifestation and demonstration of a forgiveness already assured to fallen humankind. Barth's emphasis is on God's vicarious identification with the sin and plight of humanity in Jesus Christ rather than on the satisfaction of the requirements of God's law. The themes of penal substitution and satisfaction are nonetheless present in Barth, but they are placed in a new context.

Where I have been helped most by Barth is in his fresh interpretation of biblical authority, which enables us to contend for the primacy of biblical revelation over church tradition and religious experience and at the same time acknowledge the rightful place for the historical investigation of Scripture. Barth meets and overcomes the challenge of higher criticism by showing that such criticism takes us only so far, that it must be supplemented and fulfilled by theological criticism, which is carried on only by faith seeking understanding. By positing both the priority of revelation over Scripture and their indissoluble unity by the action of the Spirit, Barth has given to the modern church an alternative that makes it possible to maintain continuity with the teaching of the church through the ages and yet be in fruitful dialogue with modernity.

Barth's criticism of natural theology is also much needed in our day when a segment of the church is appealing to new revelations in nature and history in order to justify an accommodation to some current ideology. Barth does not deny the inescapable presence of God in all creation, but he makes a convincing case that the general awareness of this divine presence cannot yield an adequate or valid knowledge of the true God, because the fall into sin warps our noetic faculties as well as corrupts our moral sensibilities.

Finally, I have benefitted from Barth's contention that ethics forms a part of dogmatics, that justification and sanctification belong together. Barth goes beyond the Reformation when he includes under the practical marks of the church *(notae ecclesiae)* obedience to the Great Commission of our Lord in addition to the preaching of the Word and the right administration of the sacraments.

Despite my indebtedness to Barth's monumental theological achievement, I have a number of reservations that have to do with content as well as with method. First, there is an unmistakable objectivistic bent in Barth's theology that tends to undercut the necessity for personal faith and repentance. Barth maintains that the proper object of theological reflection is not the relation of humanity to God in religious experience (as in Schleiermacher) but the relation of God to humanity in Jesus Christ. Against the experientialism and subjectivism that have dominated the theological scene since Schleiermacher, Barth is adamant that the basis of faith lies outside of ourselves in God's self-revelation in Jesus Christ. Our salvation, he argues, has already been enacted and fulfilled for all humankind in God's reconciling work in Jesus Christ. What remains is for us to recognize this fact and live according to it.

Consequently, says Barth, it is not the mandate of the church to call people to a decision for salvation, since salvation already extends to them because of Christ's redemptive work on the cross; instead, we should call our hearers to a decision for obedience. The response that is expected of those who hear the gospel is basically ethical rather than soteriological in significance. But does not Scripture plainly teach that only those who believe are justified and sanctified, that apart from personal faith and repentance we stand condemned in our sins (cf. Luke 13:3; John 3:18; 12:35-36; Rom. 3:22-26; 4:24-25; 10:9-11; Heb. 10:38-39)?

Reluctantly, Barth came to the conclusion that the principal enemies of true Christianity were sacramentalism and sacerdotalism, and therefore to guard against idolatry the church must emphasize the unique Lordship and freedom of Jesus Christ, the one Word of God that calls into question all other words. He acknowledged that there can be other true words of God, but these have credibility and validity only when united with and judged by the one transcendent Word—Jesus Christ. These "little lights" reflect the one great Light, Jesus Christ, but we are never to regard them as independent sources of light.

In a similar vein, Barth emphasizes the utter transcendence and uniqueness of the kingdom of God that stands over and above all movements of social reform and revolution. We cannot bring in or help to create the kingdom of God, since it is God's own creation, but we can set up signs and parables of a kingdom that is already in our midst, though hidden from the eyes of natural man. I agree with much of what Barth says in this area, but the question remains: Cannot our words and actions be instruments of the Spirit of God in his work of extending and advancing the kingdom of God? Can we as Christians only point to a kingdom that is coming, or cannot we also facilitate the coming of the kingdom by our prayers and works of mercy (cf. Acts 3:19-21; 2 Pet. 3:11-12)?

Barth's denigration of human virtue also disturbs me. While it is true that we as Christians have our righteousness in Jesus Christ by virtue of faith in his gratuitous work of redemption, are not we also called to holiness in all manner of living (1 Pet. 1:15)? Barth underplays the scriptural injunction that apart from our striving after holiness we will not see God (Heb. 12:14; Rom. 6:19; Matt. 5:8). The call to sainthood, which is an integral part of the tradition of the church catholic, is sadly neglected in his theology. According to him, only Jesus Christ is a saint and we as the people of God are saints collectively by virtue of belonging to his body. Barth regards the striving for moral excellence and sanctity with suspicion, for such striving easily fosters self-righteousness, pride in our own virtue rather than dependence on the merits of Jesus Christ alone. But cannot our striving for holiness be a sign and witness of Christ's perfect holiness? Cannot little saints be a powerful testimony of the perfect sainthood exemplified in Christ?

Barth has often been accused of teaching universalism, but he has specifically disavowed the idea of a universal homecoming *(apokatastasis)*, for this ties God to a principle. On the other hand, he does propound a universalism of hope. Because God gave his Son for the sins of the whole world and because his offer of election goes out to all, all therefore are claimed by the love of God, all are destined for the kingdom of God. We can consequently view everyone with hope, even the most unruly and despicable. Yet Barth recognizes that not all respond to this gratuitous offer: some deny and forsake the salvation assured to them through Christ's work of reconciliation and intercession. As I have indicated, Barth occasionally lapses into an objectivistic stance, suggesting that the matter of salvation is already decided. Yet there is another side to Barth's theology, which also must be taken into consideration: he explicitly declares that God is under no obligation to continue to favor those who spurn his mercy.

Despite certain imbalances in Barth's theology, I believe that he has much to say to the modern church. He is an evangelical theologian who transcends the parochialism of both fundamentalism and a narrow confessionalism. He makes a place for historical criticism; yet his writings are imbued with a love and respect for Holy Scripture as the written Word of God. He acknowledges the political implications of the gospel but refuses to tie faith to any political ideology. He continues to uphold the Calvinist vision of Christ transforming culture without falling into the kind of utopianism characteristic of liberation theology.

Theology in our time dare not avoid Barth's challenge if it is to maintain relevance and credibility. We cannot simply remain with him but must strive to go through him and beyond him (this is what he would have wanted). But we definitely cannot ignore him!

Karl Barth and Emil Brunner—A Tangled Tale with a Happy Ending (or, The Story of a Relationship)

I. John Hesselink

Introduction

The person and the theology of Karl Barth have made an indelible impact on my life. That impact, however, has been interwoven with the impact of his Swiss compatriot, Emil Brunner. What I want to share here is my involvement in their relationship with each other, particularly in the latter years of their lives.

My personal involvement with these two stretched over a period of almost a decade. As a college student in the post–World War II period and as a seminarian in the early 1950s the names of Barth and Brunner were quite familiar to me, Barth more by reputation, Brunner more directly through his writings. At Western Seminary in Holland, Michigan, we read Brunner's *The Mediator*, *The Divine Imperative*, and Volume I of his dogmatics, *The Doctrine of God*. As a senior I wrote a term paper on Barth's view of revelation, based largely on *Church Dogmatics* I/1, the only volume available in English translation at that time.

I was impressed and fascinated by both of these theological giants, but at the same time was not comfortable with everything I read. Coming from a conservative Reformed background, I was particularly concerned about their understanding of the nature of biblical authority.

In any case, little did I dream that I would ever meet either of these theologians, let alone study under them. What a pleasant surprise it was, then, to learn upon our arrival in Japan in September 1953 as missionaries, only four months after graduation from seminary, that the next month Dr. and Mrs. Brunner were due to arrive in Tokyo. Dr. Brunner was to be the first visiting professor of Christianity and Ethics at the newly formed International Christian University (ICU) in Tokyo. An announcement soon appeared in the papers that in addition to his lectures for ICU students Brunner was also going to give a series of lectures on "Christianity and Existentialism" on Saturday mornings for a more general audience. In addition, he would offer a seminar limited to twenty graduate students.

We had been assigned to Tokyo with the purpose of doing language study. Since that took place Monday through Friday, I was free on Saturdays to attend Brunner's special lectures and was also fortunate to be admitted into his seminar. This was only the beginning of a long and meaningful relationship with Emil Brunner and his family. That relationship deepened when a small group of missionaries continued to meet for informal theological discussions with Brunner at his home on the ICU campus. As families we also came to be friends.

In the spring of 1955 the Brunners returned to Zürich because of Mrs. Brunner's ill health. En route home Brunner himself suffered a stroke. Although he had already resigned his position at the University of Zürich, the effects of this stroke were to limit somewhat his subsequent physical and intellectual activities.

In the meantime, we corresponded and I pursued various possibilities for graduate study. Had Brunner still been active as a professor, I might well have done my graduate work with him. Instead, through a variety of circumstances and the encouragement of a Swiss missionary friend, the late Werner Kohler, I ended up being accepted as a doctoral candidate by none other than Karl Barth. He warned me that he wasn't sure how long he would continue at the University of Basel—it was now the spring of 1958—but that if I was willing to take that risk I should proceed. He also indicated he was very interested in my proposed thesis subject, "Calvin's Concept of the Law."

When I first broke this news to Brunner, he was angry and upset, fearing that I would become another Barthian. When I pointed out to him that I was my own man theologically and had not become a Brunnerian despite my admiration and affection for him, he relented and apologized and urged me to visit them at the soonest opportunity.

I did exactly that. After arriving in Basel in October 1958, I dropped off my belongings at the Theologisches Alumneum (operated by Oscar Cullmann and his sister), which was to be my residence for five months, and proceeded to Zürich where I spent my first weekend in Switzerland. A few days later I arranged for my first visit with Barth but said nothing about my relationship to Brunner!

Not many months later my informal role as a liaison began. Whenever I visited the Brunners (later with my wife and three small children) Brunner was always eager to know what Barth was doing in his seminars and how the *Church Dogmatics* was progressing. Occasionally he would voice misgivings about certain aspects of Barth's theology, but he also expressed great admiration for his Basel counterpart. I still recall, for example, an early conversation with Brunner as we were taking a walk. He suddenly stopped, turned to me, and said, "You know there are several outstanding theologians such as Bultmann and Tillich, but there is only one genius among us and that is Karl Barth."

Barth eventually learned about my relationship to Brunner when an American student in Basel mentioned in passing that I had led a group of theological students to Zürich to spend an evening with Brunner. Fortunately, by that time my relationship with Barth was solid enough that it did not imperil our friendship. In fact, occasionally he would ask me if I had seen Brunner recently and would ask about his welfare.

That might have been the extent of my involvement with the two—and their involvement with each other—had not Mrs. Brunner taken the initiative to do something more direct and personal. That story is told in what follows and is reproduced from *The Reformed Journal*, April 1962.

The Elephant and the Whale

In the fall of 1960 a corps of TV technicians and an announcer representing BBC of London crossed the English Channel and made their way to Switzerland. The reason: neither an international political conclave in Geneva nor a major sports event. They went rather to film and interview two of the most influential and renowned theologians of our time—Emil Brunner and Karl Barth. They spent over an hour with each man in his own home. The two interviews were presented together on one show, which was given in January 1961. The interviewer had obviously received some theological briefing, for in his interview with Barth (Brunner had been interviewed first) he concluded by posing a question which has perplexed many a theologian. He asked Barth if he could describe or explain his relationship to his near-neighbor in Zürich, Emil Brunner. The question was most appropriate, for both men had much in common: nationality, age (Barth was three years older), specific area of work (dogmatics), and geographical proximity (Zürich and Basel being only about sixty miles apart). More important, both were leaders in the theological movement known as dialectical theology or neo-orthodoxy. Yet their relationship had been marked by a strange reserve and occasionally a definite hostility. Hence the significance of Barth's half-jocular but perceptive reply.

"In his good creation," said Barth, "God saw fit to create such diverse creatures as an elephant and a whale.[1] Each has his own function and purpose. But they are so different that they cannot communicate with each other or even fight with each other. As a result, they also cannot conclude a peace pact with each other. Why God chose to place such diverse creatures in the same universe no one knows. For the answer to this question we must wait until the eschaton. Only then will it become clear as to why God created the elephant and the whale."

"That," Barth added, "may help to explain my relationship to Emil Brunner." With this the televised interview ended. The interviewer, however, could not refrain from asking afterwards, "Which, Professor Barth, would you prefer to be?" Barth paused for a moment and then replied, "I believe I would rather be a whale. An elephant is limited to the land, whereas a whale can traverse the whole creation."

Although their conflict about natural theology generated the most heat and excitement, the cleavage between the two theologians was by no means limited to that one problem. For example, in 1932, when the first volume of the monumental *Church Dogmatics* appeared, Barth gave notice in the Foreword that he was forsaking Kierkegaard and existentialist philosophy and was now taking more seriously the early church fathers, and particularly Anselm of Canterbury. Then in the second chapter of this volume he points out that Brunner and he even have a different understanding of the function and purpose of theology.

Granted, they agree in most fundamentals, but their differences are far from incidental. When they are compared to Bultmann or Tillich, they seem very close. Nevertheless, they have disagreed—and sometimes rather violently—about all of the following issues: an-

---

1. Barth had used this same metaphor earlier in describing his relationship to Rudolf Bultmann. See *Karl Barth/Rudolf Bultmann Letters 1922–1966* (ET Grand Rapids: Eerdmans, 1981), No. 95.

thropology, ethics, the church, election, the *analogia entis,* the virgin birth, and law and gospel.

This *"Auseinandersetzung,"* which went on for forty years, was rarely carried on in direct confrontation. At times their disputes were rather acrimonious, but since they were usually waged with the pen rather than orally (and at a distance of at least sixty miles), the debate never became a personal feud. The relationship, as Barth aptly illustrated in his parable, is more like that of an elephant and a whale who cannot really communicate with each other. Despite their proximity, their paths rarely crossed, and then only in an incidental sort of way. The Amsterdam Assembly of the World Council of Churches in 1948 brought them together. They next met at the Zürich airport in 1953, when Barth came to say farewell to the Brunners prior to their departure for Japan.

In view of all this, their unheralded first real "encounter" in decades, which took place on November 19, 1960, assumes special significance. The Brunners had promised us that as soon as Dr. Brunner finished the third and last volume of his *Dogmatics* they would make the "long" journey to Basel and visit us. In October 1960, Mrs. Brunner called to confirm their visit (*Dogmatik* III had just appeared). She then divulged that Dr. Brunner had suggested that since they were coming to Basel anyway, it might be nice if they paid their respects to the Barths at which time Dr. Brunner could present a copy of Volume III of his *Dogmatics* to Barth. What did I think? and if I thought this was feasible, would I make the necessary arrangements.

I had intended to discuss the matter first with Barth's secretary, Miss von Kirschbaum. I called, expecting her to reply (she usually answered the phone), but to my dismay Barth himself answered. I had no recourse but to blurt out my message. The response, however, was instantaneous, expressing both surprise and joy. His exact words were: "Ach was! ein grosses historische Ereignis," which being freely interpreted means, "Not really! this will be a great historical event."

I continued to play the role of mediator and was somewhat amused to see that as the day for the visit drew near, both parties evidenced growing anticipation and a touch of apprehension. Almost every time Barth saw me during the intervening weeks he would stop and ask if everything was still in order. He also asked if I wouldn't come along, something which the Brunners had taken for granted. The climax came on the Thursday night prior to the appointed Saturday. After one of his informal seminars, he motioned that he wanted to speak to me. His request sounds fantastic until one realizes the long silence which had marked their relationship during the past years. Barth put his hand on my shoulder and said quite earnestly, "Mr. Hesselink, you know Brunner better than I do. Tell me, what shall I say to him when he visits me?" I could not help but laugh at the ludicrousness of the situation, but it became clear that Barth was not joking. I made some tentative suggestions, and Barth concluded by noting that in any case there were two subjects which should *not* be discussed, namely, natural theology and Communism!

On the fateful day, I met the Brunners at the train station and took them to the Barths. It had been agreed on beforehand that the visit should not last more than an hour. Brunner was obviously nervous and showed more than usual the effects of his last stroke. Barth's very warm, genuine welcome at the door, however, dispelled any doubts the Brunners may have had. It was a particularly moving experience for the two wives who had not seen each other in forty years! The first attempts at conversation were a bit awkward, something like two teenagers on their first date. But soon the wives were engaged in enthusiastic conversation and eventually the men also entered into a free, vigorous discussion of matters which were rather theological. Barth's secretary, Miss von Kirschbaum, was the only other person present and she began to chat with me, so I could not follow the whole conversation.

At noon, as Mrs. Brunner proposed that they should leave, Barth turned to me, winked, and said, "We were just discussing Communism!" I smiled, turned to the Brunners and said, "Yes, we had better be going."

Despite a light drizzle, the two men posed happily for several snapshots. It was the first time they had been photographed together since the Amsterdam Assembly. Even more touching than the greetings were the farewells. As we drove away, Barth stood on the curb waving fondly until we were out of sight. His countenance was absolutely cherubic.

After dinner, a nap, and a visit in our apartment, the Brunners returned to Zürich. While eating and visiting there was little occasion to discuss the "encounter," but en route to the station Mrs. Brunner finally asked her husband just what they had discussed. Brunner thought for a moment, then laughed and said, "You know, I hardly remember anything."

But that is not quite the end of the story. Soon afterwards queries came from both quarters about the reactions of the other party. The Brunners were overjoyed that their "daring move" had come off so successfully and were grateful that Barth had felt the same way. When Barth learned of Brunner's reactions, he expressed what obviously was the feeling on both sides. He beamed and said benignly, "Ah, now I am at peace."

Some people who heard about this event asked if a real reconciliation took place. The answer is no, for two reasons. Theologically this was impossible. As Barth said prior to the encounter, "Too much water has flowed under the bridge." Personally, no reconciliation took place because none was necessary. Whatever distaste they might have had for each other's theological positions on certain points, there was no deep personal enmity. Nevertheless, this experience obviously meant a great deal to both of the distinguished theologians. As Brunner had implied to his wife in his reply to her, *what* they said was not important. Far more important was the fact *that* they had stopped writing about each other and had finally gotten together to talk like Christian gentlemen. For theologians too are sinful people with strange quirks and funny foibles, people who like everyone else stand in the need of understanding and forgiveness.

The Aftermath—From *Nein* to *Ja*

As it turned out, this encounter between Barth and Brunner was to be their last time together this side of heaven.

In June 1961, having completed my dissertation and oral examinations, we left Basel and returned to Japan via the United States. Prior to this I had received an invitation to teach historical theology at Tokyo Union Seminary, a position I held from November 1961 until May 1973, when we returned to the States and I became president of Western Theological Seminary in Holland, Michigan.

I continued to correspond with both Barth and Brunner, albeit infrequently due to the press of my new responsibilities. I did become involved, however, in an interesting event relating to each of them. In the fall of 1963, an English daily newspaper in Tokyo, *The Asahi Evening News,* wanted to run a major feature on the Christian attitude toward peace. From the Japanese side they asked my colleague, Dr. Hidenobu Kuwada, president of Tokyo Union Seminary, to write a major presentation. Then at Kuwada's instigation, they asked Barth for a response. I acted as the middleman in these negotiations and edited the English translations of both contributions (the substance of Barth's response is found in Letter No. 74 in *Karl Barth, Letters 1961–1968* [Grand Rapids: Eerdmans, 1981]).

In the spring of 1966 I suddenly received a long-distance telephone call from Mrs. Brunner asking whether I would be willing to act as Dr. Brunner's representative and accept an honorary degree that was about to be conferred on him by the International Christian University at their opening spring convocation. She explained that Dr. Brunner was not well and could not personally make the trip to Tokyo to receive this degree. Thus I "stood in," so to speak, for Brunner at the ICU convocation and later shared with the Brunners the highlights of the day.

Already at this time I was eagerly looking forward to renewing my friendship with both of my theological mentors, for we were due for a furlough beginning in June 1966. Unfortunately, Brunner died prior to our departure but we did visit Mrs. Brunner upon our arrival in Switzerland in July. Among other things, she related how kind and caring Barth had been during the last months of her husband's illness. Barth himself had experienced health problems earlier that spring and had not been able to make a trip to Zürich, but he had offered the services of his personal physician who apparently was a specialist in the area of Brunner's illness (cancer of the prostrate gland), an offer that touched the Brunners.

Barth was not in Basel at that time but was spending a few weeks with his wife at a chalet in Arbaz that belonged to Madam Frommel, their son Christoph's mother-in-law. I contacted them by telephone and Barth urged me to visit them if possible. A date was set and when I arrived early on a warm, humid afternoon, I was greeted warmly by Mrs. Barth. She explained that her husband was napping but would soon be up. A few moments later Barth entered the living room and after asking about the family, paused and said, "Well, our friend Emil Brunner is no longer with us." Then he briefly reflected on his relationship to Brunner and expressed regret that it had not been possible to visit him again before his death. (In retrospect it occurred to me that neither Mrs. Brunner nor he mentioned his last letter to Brunner, included below.) Then we discussed a variety of subjects, such as the autobiography he was writing, but he admitted he was only up to his grandparents!

I returned to Basel later that afternoon. That was the last time I was to see Professor Barth. What was striking about that visit was that the first thing Barth wanted to discuss with me was Brunner's death. Granted, that was a recent event, but I did not initiate the conversation and we had not seen each other in five years! Apparently, seeing me immediately triggered this reaction since he associated me with Brunner and their last encounter.

This is significant, I feel, and indirectly answers the question I have been asked countless times, "Did their historic encounter in November 1960 effect a real reconciliation?" My answer to that question is usually a dialectical "yes and no." No, in the sense that nothing was resolved theologically. Despite all they believed in common, their theological differences were too great to be resolved in a few hours, if at all. Yes, in the sense that it restored a personal contact and communication that had been broken. It obviously meant a lot to them personally, both at the time of the meeting and in the following years.

Some have not seen it the same way, though. For example, Eberhard Busch wrote the following in his biography of Barth:

> Another contemporary with whom Barth now sought unsuccessfully to reach an understanding was his Zürich colleague Emil Brunner. A reunion arranged at the Bruderholz on 19 November 1960 by the American missionary to Japan, John Hessclink, who had just gained his doctorate in Basel, ended disappointingly.[2]

Likewise, the encounter has been described as "an unnecessary and sentimental piece of ecumenism."[3] This is not the place, however, to dwell on various interpretations. The important thing, in my mind, is that Barth viewed the encounter in a positive light, which is further corroborated by his approval of having the incident related in *How I Changed My Mind*,[4] published the following year by John Godsey, a former student of Barth's. In the epilogue, "Barth's Life After 1958," Godsey tells about the encounter at some length and notes: "Although both couples approached the encounter with considerable apprehension, the occasion turned out to be a most enjoyable one which succeeded, not in reconciling theological differences, but in clearing the air and cementing personal relationships" (p. 77). This puts the matter very well and places it in proper perspective, I believe.

---

2. Eberhard Busch, *Karl Barth*, trans. John Bowden (Philadelphia: Fortress Press, 1976), p. 449.

3. T. H. L. Parker, *Karl Barth* (Grand Rapids: Eerdmans, 1970), p. 99.

4. A collection of essays that had previously appeared under this title in *The Christian Century* over several decades; ed. John D. Godsey (Atlanta: John Knox Press, 1966).

On the one hand, the friendship, though strained at times, was never broken. On the other, theological differences continued to haunt their relationship down to the very end of their days. It may be this factor to which Busch alludes when he says that the historic encounter "ended disappointingly," for three years after the meeting (November 11, 1963) Barth wrote a letter to Brunner's son, Hans Heinrich, a pastor in Zürich, lamenting the fact that his father was still repeating certain old charges in his latest book, the new edition of *Wahrheit als Begegnung* (1963; ET *Truth as Encounter*). Barth's purpose in writing was to see if H. H. Brunner might not discretely influence his father in this regard. Barth wrote:

> I am a little disturbed by what your father has written about me in the new edition of *Wahrheit als Begegnung*, pp. 45f.; every statement is a wild distortion, and that after I had thought he and I could end our days in a kind of truce. [Then a footnote is appended by the editors: "A personal reconciliation had taken place between Barth and Brunner in November, 1960."] Could this not be discontinued or prevented? . . . I thought that I should at least tell you that I take no pleasure in this rekindling of ancient anger.[5]

H. H. Brunner apparently responded quickly to Barth and in a sensitive, sympathetic fashion, for Barth responded on November 21 with a letter (No. 129) expressing great appreciation for his efforts.

The next recorded correspondence with a member of the Brunner family is to Emil Brunner himself. Dated October 26, 1964 (No. 169), it is a warm note of thanks to Brunner for expressing his concern in regard to Barth's recent illness. Here the tone is clearly that of a friend, not of a theological foe. Among other things Barth writes, "When I am on my feet again, I will watch out for the first opportunity to visit you, as I have planned to do for a time." This good intention, unfortunately, was never realized.

Barth sent only one more letter directly to Brunner. This one, dated January 29, 1965 (No. 175), is again a response to a sympathy note from Brunner along with Brunner's last published piece, a little book on the Swiss novelist, Gottfried Keller. Here Barth's irenic side and obvious desire not to rekindle the old flames of animosity are beautifully evident; for in this book Brunner alludes to the signifi-

---

5. This letter is No. 128 in *Karl Barth. Letters 1961–1968*, trans. Geoffrey W. Bromiley (Grand Rapids: Eerdmans, 1981), p. 140. Further references to letters are from this book.

cance of conscience for Keller from the standpoint of natural theology. In earlier days this would have triggered a fiery blast from Barth; but now Barth simply notes that although he has "lost all sympathy" for Keller and has doubts about his use of eros and conscience, he wants Brunner to "note that I am not making any polemical observations regarding p. 33. So mild have I become in my old age!"

Approximately a year later, Brunner became seriously ill. Barth accordingly no longer corresponds directly with Brunner but with his wife and with his pastor, Pfarrer Peter Vogelsanger of the Fraumunster Church in Zürich. In his letter to Mrs. Brunner on March 7, 1966 (No. 204), in response to her letter telling of her husband's condition, Barth wrote: "Your letter and the two appended lines by Emil touched me very much" (the original German is even stronger: "hat mich sehr bewegt"). Then Barth expressed a sentiment based on one of his favorite texts, 2 Corinthians 1:18ff.: "Tell him the time is long past when I shout No to him or anybody. We all can and should be glad to have a God who without any merits on our part says Yes to each of us in his own way." After a very personal paragraph in which Barth reflects on their respective situations and urges Brunner to live by the promise "Blessed are those who mourn, for they shall be comforted," he concludes, "If only I were a little better I would come over to exchange a few words with Emil. Greet him from me and greetings to yourself, dear Mrs. Brunner."

Obviously the old warrior no longer wants to do battle with his old friend who has also been his nemesis. To the contrary, there is a compassion and tenderness that is not matched by any other letters in this volume—and several of them are very touching.

The next letter Barth received concerning Brunner's condition was from Brunner's pastor and close friend, Peter Vogelsanger, who had written a long letter to Barth on April 2, apprising him of Brunner's failing condition. Barth, sensing that Brunner's days were numbered, responded by return mail. The letter (No. 207) is brief; the two main paragraphs deserve to be quoted in full:

> If I were more active after my two-year illness I would take the next train to press Emil Brunner's hand again.
>
> If he is still alive and it is possible, tell him that I commend him to *our* God. And tell him the time when I thought I should say No to him is long since past, and we all live only by the fact that a great and merciful God speaks his gracious Yes to all of us.

This letter, like the one sent to Mrs. Brunner a month earlier, is beautiful and moving in its own right; but when one knows the context in which it was received, it takes on an even deeper meaning. The editors appended this note:

> Vogelsanger received Barth's letter the morning of 5 April, rushed to the hospital, where Brunner was weak but alive and conscious, and read the letter with Barth's greeting. A slight but beautiful smile came over Brunner's features and he quietly pressed Vogelsanger's hand. A few minutes later Brunner went into a coma from which he did not awake, dying peacefully near midday on 6 April. Barth's seems to have been his last earthly greeting.

Postscript

The story does not quite end here, for there is one more letter that finally concludes the Barth–Brunner relationship, a letter of condolence to Mrs. Brunner (No. 209). The intriguing thing about the letter is that Barth is still haunted by the past and is seeking to achieve a clearer understanding of his checkered relationship with Brunner. After expressing his sympathy, he admits this concern:

> Naturally I have been considering, too, the question how it really was, and how it came to be, between him and me. How glad I would be to have you tell me personally and orally how our relation appeared from his and your standpoint. From my standpoint the fact was that God not only led him and me on very different paths, but in his unfathomable goodness and wisdom willed us already to be very different people [shades of the elephant and whale parable!—IJH]— so different that properly there would be no question at all of strife or suffering between us. And yet we did strive and suffer on both sides. And if I am right he suffered more at my hands than I did at his, once I had let off steam [meinen Kropf einmal geleart hatte!] in 1934. . . .
>
> I write all this because I am almost eighty years old and would like to have as clear as possible a picture of my responsibility in relation to this part of my past. . . .

Four months later we visited Mrs. Brunner. In the midst of her sorrow she was also still glowing because of these last moving exchanges with Barth. And as Pfarrer Herrmann recently shared with me (June 1985), during his last days on this earth Barth testified concerning his sense of peace in regard to the Brunners.

The time of acrimony and accusations is past; the negatives *(nein)* are now replaced by affirmations *(ja)*, both human and divine.

Barth and Berlin: Theology at the Wall

Harvey Cox

When I landed in Templehof airdrome in August 1962, one year after the erection of the Wall, I discovered that the city had another Great Divide. It was the gap between the Barthians and the Bultmannians among the Protestant pastors and theologians.

I had arrived in Berlin at the age of thirty-three to serve for one year as an "Ecumenische Mitarbeiter"—usually translated in English as "Ecumenical Fraternal Worker." By means of a complex set of arrangements I was paid by American Baptists, designated by the World Council of Churches, assigned to the Evangelical Church of Berlin-Brandenburg (then still presided over by the aging Bishop Otto Dibelius), placed at the disposal of the Gossner Mission, which had both an East and West headquarters, and then actually posted "dadrybne" in Gossner's East Berlin program on the "other side" of the bracks and barbed wire. Thanks to the mysterious intricacies of the Four Power Agreement by which Berlin was then governed, I was allowed to travel to the East Sector from my residence in the Friedenau district of West Berlin, through either Checkpoint Charley or S-Bahn Alexanderplatz on a daily basis, since I held an American passport. I just had to be sure I returned to the West every day before midnight. To make matters a little more complicated, Pastor Bruno Schottstadt, who then headed the Gossner Mission's operation in East Berlin, thought that in addition to teaching in the Lay Theological Education program I should also attend the weekly meetings of Unterwegs Ost, a lively theological discussion group consisting of East German pastors and teachers, and also spend whatever time I could at the East German Evangelical Academy located in the northern suburb of Weisensee.

I spent the year as a commuter between two worlds. Wherever I went, however, I quickly learned that whatever else might be complicated, one thing was quite simple: no matter which side of the Wall one worked on, to be on the right side theologically meant to be for Karl and against Rudolf.

This was not a hard stance for me to take. Raised in a pietistic evangelical setting where subjective feelings about the faith were unduly central, my reading of Barth in seminary classes at Yale under the tutelage of Claude Welch had been both an enlightenment and a liberation. I became (and, some will claim, have never ceased entirely to be) a "Barthian." Here was theology which in its essential ingredients sounded like the "right stuff" I had been raised on doctrinally, but shorn of both the sentimentalism and the quasi-fundamentalism. The conversion Barth produced in me was so thoroughgoing that I stalwartly informed the Baptist ordination council that reviewed my case—an already dubious one due to my suspect education at a "liberal" seminary—that I chose not to write the customary required essay describing "my religious experience." What was important, I told the council with fresh-out-of-seminary self-assurance, was not *my* experience but what *Das Wort Gottes* actually said. This puzzled the more pietistically inclined members of the council, but it elicited nods of approval from the Bible carriers. I was approved for ordination, but only by a very close vote.

Berlin in 1962 was not the first time or place I found myself in a strife-torn area where a full-scale theological battle was underway with no quarter given. When I came to Harvard in the fall of 1958 to pursue my doctoral studies, the turf was divided between the disciples of St. Karl and the groupies of St. Paul (Tillich). The fact that Tillich was actually on the scene holding seminars and classes did not seem to afford his cadres any visible advantage. I vividly remember Tillich's advanced seminar, which met at his home on Chauncey Street. The great man, giant safety-pin "totem" in hand, would preside genially over almost any student presentation. But when the candidate ventured to explicate this or that theme from the *Church Dogmatics* (such as "The concept of *Wirkliches Mensch,*" as one student did) Tillich would rest his brow on his hand, finger the totem more energetically, and restrict his comments to saying that he found it hard to speak about a theology that had such naive and uncritical philosophical presuppositions. A queasy silence usually followed this remark. We all remembered that when one student had sought to explain to Tillich (who had come to Harvard at President Nathan Pusey's invitation after his retirement from Union) that Barth's whole point was that we should not try to evaluate theology from a philosophical vantage point, the gray retiree from Manhattan had simply shaken his lionine head and muttered disconsolately that, in that case, "everything since Aristotle is lost."

The bivouac area for the followers of Barth at Harvard in those days were the seminars that Paul Lehmann ran on the still untranslated volumes of *Kirchliche Dogmatik*. Lehmann was scrupulous, demanding, acerbic, and scintillating. There was a heady feeling in the seminar not unmixed with a bit of elitism since those of us who were working through hundreds of pages of German text felt we had the right to enjoy at least a slight sense of superiority over the dullards who had not progressed that far in their teutonic vocabulary building and verb identification. But there was something else that attracted us to Barth at the time. What was it? Something tensile, luminous, bracing—almost inspiring—kept us in his grip. Cracking open one of those bulky, light-brown volumes of the *KD* and swimming in the long sentences, clinging now and then to a historical footnote like rocks in a torrent: it all had something of the magic the poet once felt upon first opening Chapman's Homer. Even better, we were getting it in the original. Even though we did not know why at times—maybe most of the time—we somehow sensed we were splashing in a stream that had arisen from primal cisterns and was flowing toward a Somewhere that was important. Tasting the triumph of grace, we were a little intoxicated and a little cocky. Come to think of it, I cannot really blame Tillich for not appreciating us all that much. In retrospect he seems to have been more generous than I would have been under the circumstances.

It is true that by the time I got to Berlin in 1962 I was no longer—if I had ever really been—a pure Barthian. One person who had led me astray, even pulled me toward the Tillich camp, was James Luther Adams, my main doctoral advisor. Adams had translated some of the first of Tillich's writings to appear in English, many of which appeared in *The Protestant Era*. Although Adams was very fond of Paul Lehmann and they taught a memorable seminar on Ernst Troeltsch together, he had little liking for Barth's theology. Studying with Adams and reading some of Tillich's razor sharp essays in *The Protestant Era*, I became something of a maverick by the time I finished my Ph.D. I still resonated with the toughness and cogency of Barth as opposed to what increasingly appeared to me to be a kind of obsession for inclusiveness, an awful need to stretch the tent larger and larger to hold all the animals in Tillich's later writings. But I liked Adams's "early Tillich" and I resonated with the politics of *The Protestant Era*, the attack on capitalism, the brilliant reading of Marx, the inspired decoding of the meaning of modernity. The Barth that came through the *Church Dogmatics* seemed disturbingly depoliticized to me. I did not know it at the time, but I was ready for the very political Barth I would meet in Berlin, especially in the person of a young assistant professor at the Kirchliche Hochschule named Frederich-Wilhelm Marquardt.

It was not the first time Marquardt and I had met. In 1957, on my honeymoon, my new bride and I had visited Berlin. Since I was then the Campus Minister at Oberlin College we were housed in a student guest house at the Free University of Berlin. Marquardt was the Student Pastor at the time. We met and talked. When I got back to Berlin in 1962 I looked him up and found that he attended meetings of the Unterwegs West, the West Berlin equivalent of the group I belonged to in the East. (Since Berliners were not permitted to cross the Wall at that time from either direction, the two groups could not visit each other and I soon became a kind of courier.) It was Marquardt who explained to me why Barth had become the *lingua franca* of the politically engaged theologians of Berlin, both East and West. The real theological question, as he saw it, was not Bultmann's "modern man" or the disappearance of the mythical worldview. Rather, it was the question of justice and, even more, of peace. He saw Barth as what I would now call a "postmodern" theologian.

Living in Berlin meant peace was literally a daily issue. We were reminded every day of what war does to a people and a city and that a new war could break out at any moment. Through the center of the downtown area a stone and wire barrier severed house from house, neighborhood from neighborhood. We knew, although we tried not to think about it all the time, that we lived on a kind of island. One had only to drive to one of the tiny lakes on the edge of town and take an accidental wrong turn on the way home to be reminded that the Wall not only cut us off from friends and family in the East. It also completely surrounded West Berlin.

But for the Christians I knew, in both East and West, it was not useful or even accurate to blame the Wall on the communists. The petty Stalinist bureaucrats who had ordered its construction had merely been putting the final seal on a conflictual history that went back to the Versailles Treaty, the subverting of the Weimar Republic, the rise of the Nazis, the war and the capitulation, the falling out of the victorious powers, the present stalemate. All Christians I met in Berlin had a strong sense of vocation. They believed they were called to live in that divided city; to bear witness to God's love for believers and unbelievers alike; to insist that because God has chosen to be the God who is with us and for us, we are free to choose to be with and for our neighbors, even the atheists.

If this all sounds very much like the language of Barth, there is good reason. It was Barth who provided the theological bread and butter for us in Berlin in those days. His theology was a warning against self-righteousness. It assured us that the communist functionaries we met and argued with and beside whom we lived were also included in God's sweeping "election" of all people. Occasionally I was able to slip copies of books into the East on my trips over. What the pastors and teachers and lay people wanted most were copies of the *Kirchliche Dogmatik*. To carry in something by Bultmann would have been a wasted risk. Let the bourgeois preachers in West Germany agonize about the disappearance of the three-decker universe and existentialism. We had weightier matters to confront. "Jesus Christ died," as Heinemann had said—in the spirit of Barth—"not against Communism but *for* all people."

There was something else about the Berliner's Barth that attracted me. As far back as 1963 I remember Marquardt telling me that one had to understand all of Barth's theological corpus from the perspective of his commitment to socialism. This political perspective, Marquardt said, was neither derivative nor accidental. It was fundamental and prior. It was Barth's *sitz im leben*. What Barth was writing, he said, was really a kind of political theology. It was Marquardt who first pointed out this paragraph in CD to me:

> For this reason the human righteousness required by God and established in obedience—the righteousness which according to Amos 5:24 should pour down as a mighty stream—has necessarily the character of a vindication of right in favour of the threatened innocent, the oppressed poor, widows, orphans and aliens. For this reason, in the relations and events in the life of His people, God always takes His stand unconditionally and passionately on this side and on this side alone: against the lofty and on behalf of the lowly; against those who already enjoy right and privilege and on behalf of those who are denied and deprived of it. What does all this mean? It is not really to be explained by talking *in abstracto* of the political tendency and especially the forensic character of the Old Testament and the biblical message generally. It does in fact have this character and we cannot hear it and believe it without feeling a sense of responsibility in the direction indicated. (II/1, 386)

A number of years later I read Gustavo Gutiérrez's first little essay, "Points Toward a Theology of Liberation," which he wrote originally for a meeting of a World Council of Churches program called SODEPAX (I think the initials stand for something having to do with the participation of the churches in development). This essay was later lengthened into his book, *Theology of Liberation*. When I read it, I was ready; and I had been made ready by the Barth I got to know in the shadow of the Wall, from the pastors and ordinary Christians who lived bravely in Berlin during those hard but heady days and who seemed to know with some wonderful assurance that they were just where God wanted them to be. For me, the step from Barth to liberation theology was a natural and easy one.

The Barth I met in Berlin also launched me on another path whose end is not yet in sight. Berlin, after all, is the city of Bonhoeffer. Granted, Barth and Bonhoeffer had their differences. Barth, some say, considered Bonhoeffer to be something of a young show-off and smart aleck. And when Bonhoeffer came to Basel during the war to sound Barth out on getting through to the allies from the German underground, there was something about his attitude that upset the older man. Nonetheless, for at least one theologian in Berlin, Bonhoeffer represented the only logical and historically creditable outcome of Barth's work. That was Hanfried Müller.

Müller at that time was a young professor at the theological faculty of the Humboldt University in East Berlin. He was a loyal and vociferous member of Unterwegs Ost and a stalwart follower of Barth. A man with an amazingly complicated way of talking, he often introduced comments into the discussion at Unterwegs meetings that lost me after a few long and convoluted sentences. Nonetheless, upon my arrival in Berlin, Pastor Schottstadt had presented me a copy of Müller's book about Bonhoeffer, *Von der Kirche zur Welt*. I had tried to read it but found it just too difficult, especially in the early months when my German was still weak. Still, the title intrigued me, as did some of the comments Müller made at Unterwegs Ost. Behind the linguistic pyrotechnics he seemed to be talking about something I had kept wondering about. How could Barth's "Church Theology" become a theology of and for and about the world? How could I get it to do for me now what *The Protestant Era* had once done?

Finally, I actually read Müller's book. A light went on. I began to study Bonhoeffer himself in earnest. I had already read *The Cost of Discipleship* and *Prisoner for God*. I had found the first too pious, the second fascinating but theologically no more than a handful of hints. But, pushed by Müller's book and the spirit of Dietrich himself, which seemed to hover over Tegel and Zehlendorf in those days, I was launched into the love and admiration for Bonhoeffer that has never left me. I agree with Barth that he was something of a smart aleck. But I have also come to agree with Müller that he really picked up the essential ingredients of Barth's thought and carried them as far as they would go, even though Gutiérrez thinks that was not quite far enough (sec his final essay in *The Power of the Poor in History*). From Müller and Bonhoeffer and Berlin I became convinced that I wanted to write a theological essay that would go "Von der Kirche zur Welt." I wanted to take what Barth had taught me and look at American culture—at *Playboy*, John F. Kennedy, the civil rights movement, the Miss America Pageant, the city—from that angle. When I came back from Berlin in 1963 I wanted to put all this together, so I started to write. I once considered calling my book *From the Church to the World*, but I decided that might be misunderstood. So I called it *The Secular City*. Those who read between its lines have commented (some in a complaining tone) that it relies heavily on Barth. It does.

When I left Berlin some of my friends there gave me a photo album. Even now I look through it at times. It brings back rich, warm memories. It even includes a picture I clipped out of a church magazine that shows Bonhoeffer standing in the prison yard of Tegel, looking remarkably dapper if not exactly smart alecky (it was before he transferred to the Gestapo prison). There are no pictures of Barth in my album. But when I close it and think about that eventful year, his spirit seems to inhabit the Friederichstrasse, the Kaiser Wilhelm Church, the Marienkirche, Weisensee, the Bundesalle—all the places I met with my, and his, friends—just as it did then. Barth was not in Berlin the year I lived there, not physically, anyway. But it was there I came to know him, really know him, for the first time.

An Appreciation of Karl Barth

Langdon Gilkey

This will be a personal rather than a scholarly appreciation of Karl Barth, a brief chronicle of my own intellectual relation to this, the greatest theologian of our century. Strangely, even though I was certainly one of those in the second generation who were personally most deeply moved and intellectually transformed by the Krisis or dialectical theology (what we in America call, I think rightly, neo-orthodoxy), the first years of my theological existence were almost completely void of direct Barthian influence. Since this is, I presume, somewhat unusual for that period, perhaps I had best begin with an explanation.

As France was falling in the spring of 1940—my college senior year—I heard Reinhold Niebuhr preach and was immediately "grasped" by the power and validity of his theological interpretation of our desperate historical situation. I will not here describe the anatomy of that desperation but merely record that suddenly and for the first time to me the Christian faith not only made sense in itself but even more made sense of that situation and so of our historical existence generally. That mutual correlation of theological inter-pretation and historical situation has remained fundamental for my theology ever since. In any case, previously, as a college major in philosophy, I had made contact neither with theology nor with the-ologians; literally I had never heard of Augustine, nor were the great names of twentieth-century theology ever mentioned (Harvard *had* no religion department). That summer (1940) I took four of Niebuhr's books from the 1930s to China with me, devoured and studied them and wrote home for more. A year later my father sent Vol. I of *The Nature and Destiny of Man,* and I practically memo-rized it. During the subsequent war (1941-45) I borrowed copies of Brunner's *Man in Revolt, The Mediator,* and *The Divine Imperative* from an Anglican missionary—and read and reread them (along with the New Testament and the six volumes of Toynbee's *Study of History*).

This was all the theology I was even acquainted with, much less knew, when I entered Union in the fall of 1946 in search of a Ph.D. in theology. Barth, therefore, was to me only a numinous name, like that of Irenaeus, Augustine, or Calvin, a giant continuously referred to and argued with but still utterly obscure. I was like someone who knew inch by inch one room (marked anthropology) in a vast palace, but who had hardly even glimpsed the rest. As a consequence, there was so much in biblical studies and historical theology, not to mention philosophy of religion and ethics, that in graduate school I had to absorb quickly (three years) that another contemporary theologian (even Barth) did not even make my first list. Although my personal concerns remained fixed on contemporary issues, professionally I thought I had to rush by present-day figures to get some control on the biblical and historical roots of twentieth-century theology. Besides, with Tillich and Niebuhr both at Union, there was more than enough current theology to absorb. It was only when I read for my thesis on the idea of Creation in juxtaposition to Bradley and Whitehead that I absorbed any Barth—but that was only, so to speak, in passing and for another purpose. My ten years at Vanderbilt immersed in historical theology did not change this pattern of trying to cover everything but twentieth-century theology. Thus it was not until the middle sixties, when I found myself at the University of Chicago responsible for modern and contemporary Protestant theology (I was then almost fifty), that I read Barth with any care—and felt for myself the vast power of which everyone else had spoken.

One consequence of this strange history (is it appropriate in an article celebrating Barth, to ascribe my very late introduction to him to Providence?) is that I have never considered myself a Barthian. Although there is little question that the fundamental shape of my theology has been generally "neo-orthodoxy," Barth had no role in *forming* that theological point of view. In fact, during those early formative years (1945–1965), whenever I would glance at one or another of his books (e.g., The Gifford Lectures in 1948), I had to admit that I did not *really* know what he was talking about. Since there were few if any historical, social, political, or existential references, I had little sense of what his theological talk *meant*. It seemed to me then empty and "mythological," unrelated to anything I felt to be "real." Later, when I had developed from historical theology more feel for purely theological problems and their importance, his thought became real to me and communicated powerfully. Still, I must admit that to this day I find myself more directly at home with theologies that continually refer to experience, personal or social, in explicating the meaning of their symbols. And even now I am not at all sure what *I* am talking about whenever my theological analyses transcend or ignore the stuff of concrete experience. It is, I suppose, because of this personal history of being "neo-orthodox" for two decades or more and yet *not* Barthian, that I have always resisted *defining* dialectical or neo-orthodox theology in exclusively Barthian terms—as so many have recently been inclined to do who, now that Brunner, the Niebuhrs, Aulén, and even Bultmann have slipped into "history," have encountered only Barth in their study of early twentieth-century theology.

It is, therefore, only in the past two decades that Barth has impinged heavily on my theological consciousness. Since I lead a seminar on his thought every two or three years, I read in him now fairly continually although I have by no means worked my way through the entire corpus. But each time I open one of his volumes, I am reminded of my reaction when I first read him carefully in about 1965: "There is no arguing with this man *while* you are reading him—his thought has entirely too much dominating or overwhelming power. If you wish to dispute with him, close the book, lock it in a closet and move away—preferably quite out of the house. Then and only then can you succeed in constructing a critique!" Few of the present students who study him agree with him wholeheartedly— but even fewer are immune to his power and influence once they get into his thought. Last spring (1985) I had intended to teach a seminar on Whitehead. However, several graduate students requested that I change the seminar to Barth. I agreed to put it to a vote among the Divinity School's theological candidates. To my surprise, it came out two to one for Barth. That would not have happened from 1940– 1965 when Whitehead reigned unchallenged at Chicago! What else this shift means, I do not know—except that it is a tribute to Barth's continuing power as a theologian.

When in introducing Barth (or ruminating about this tribute) I have asked myself what within his theology I have found most powerful (that is, most original or novel and yet true, most unexpected and yet obvious, most challenging and upsetting and yet quickly adopted), I have found myself citing the five following points. I do not list them as representing any "essence" of Barth, a full description of the heart of his theology; I list them only as what has intrigued, challenged, and influenced me in my theology.

1. First, there is his startling originality and along with that his incredible "nerve" or theological courage. You never know what he is going to say about an issue until he says it (as in revelation itself, actuality precedes possibility!); and when he says it, it always comes as a vast surprise. Further, without a visible tremor he will charge ahead against the entire history of theology, the vast battery of orthodoxy—and act as if what he says is not only obvious but orthodox! His reputation among those who have not read him is that of the champion of orthodoxy. On the contrary, over and over he turns the orthodox tradition on its head, delights in seeing crucial traditional symbols with an utterly new eye (e.g., his interpretation of predestination and of the source of evil) and in arguing endlessly and with unequalled erudition, how all the important authorities back him up! The vitality, creativity, originality, and "guts" of this man are breathtaking.

2. I am impressed with his uncanny "feel" for our cultural and historical situation; his radar set for the realities of our epoch was the most finely tuned of any writer I know, philosophical or religious. Often he is pictured as the greatest of the unmodern men, a leader among those who reject or at least look away from the modern age to ideas and viewpoints we have all long since "gone beyond." This too is absolutely wrong. He understood modernity long before most philosophers and other theologians did; he saw its intellectual and moral dilemmas, the collapse of its confidence in rationality and goodness, even its sense of helplessness and fatedness, with great clarity while most were still dreaming of civilization's control over its destiny and so of progress. And he saw the lostness and the drive toward death and self-destruction that have gradually unfolded before our eyes since that time: philosophically in positivism, existentialism, and now in deconstruction, and historically in the crises of a technological civilization, of the environment, and of nuclear power. Such a vision was not Barth's alone in 1917-18, but it was rare; and his articulation of it was, and remains, the most thorough and powerful of all. Far from "old fashioned," his was the most sophisticated and "modern"—and thoroughly learned in modern intellectual, literary, and artistic accomplishments—of all the theological (and to me the philosophical as well) minds of our culture.

3. No one has ever had a more thorough and irresistible (unarguable-against), apprehension of the *priority* of God, of God's actions and so of revelation and grace in all sound theology. This theme runs through every sentence he writes from *Romans* through his latest

works, and (to me) it creates the genuine excitement, even ecstasy, we feel when we finally "get" what it is he is saying. It is, of course, the center of his Christological center; but (for me) it is most precisely put in his apodictic rule that for good theology the actuality of revelation must *always* precede and be the basis for any talk of the "potentiality" of hearing, speaking, believing, trusting, and obeying. He is right that this is *right:* if there is a God who creates and saves, *this* is the proper way to speak obediently and truly of such a God. Few can argue successfully with this point—though almost everyone else shies away from the astonishing theological consequences that Barth draws out from this, his central principle. I am not sure how well Barth unites this principle with his recognition—as a "modern"—of the initiative, creativity, and "freedom" of the human respondent. But there is little question that he understands better than any other in this century (possibly even since the Reformation) the priority, the utter groundlessness, and the ultimate triumph of God's grace.

4. For one devoted to theology, to proclamation, to church, and to the life of faith, Barth was incredibly *realistic* about religion. Here lies perhaps his greatest break with *both* orthodoxy and liberalism: the whole paraphernalia of religious observance, belief, and even experiencing (in either its orthodox or its liberal forms) is ultimately "useless"; in fact it represents a powerful snare for the unwary, the prime locus for the human rebellion against grace. To many of us this unrelieved critique of religion at all levels and in all its phases becomes in the end inconsistent and self-defeating if carried as far as he carried it; and surely such an unqualified critique is of little help in understanding, appreciating, and learning from other religions, as we now find ourselves called to do. But Barth's "hermeneutic of suspicion" vis á vis religion, his distinction between the forms and practices of religion (even of our own) and something else (to him "revelation"—note the line is *not* drawn between outward practices and inward faith!) and so his effort always to go *beyond* the religious embodiment to its divine source is not only valid theology but, paradoxically, very helpful (if analogically used) in the present encounter of and dialogue between religions.

5. The most "modern" aspect of Barth, paradoxically united to what is most traditional—that is, the centering of all salvation on Jesus Christ—is his universalism. I find his clarity and breadth and absolute originality here endlessly inspiring. To me, something like this represents the only possible way to interpret Christian faith, that

is, in terms of the universality, the priority, the all-encompassing character, and the triumph of God's redeeming love. It is also the only basis on which a Christian can genuinely enter into dialogue with other religions—although this was (I am sure) hardly what Barth had in mind! The paradoxical greatness of the man is brightly illuminated here. At the very point where today his theology seems most "parochial"—explicitly centered in and concerned for the biblical history, its tribulations and triumphs—at that *same* point it suddenly bursts into transcendence and glory and includes, as few other viewpoints do, the furthest reaches of God's creaturely domain.

A Jewish Perspective on Karl Barth

Michael Wyschogrod

As I reflect on Karl Barth's influence on my theological development, I am forced to ask what influence Christian theology in general has had on my thinking. Such a question does not arise for a Christian theologian but it must be asked by a Jew who has spent considerable time studying Christian theology and particularly the thought of Karl Barth. From time to time, I have been called a Jewish Barthian and I have not exerted myself unduly to deny this charge. Thus a bit of explanation may be in order.

I was born in 1928 into an Orthodox Jewish home in Berlin. German Orthodoxy combined intense loyalty to Torah observance with considerable Western acculturation. It was taken for granted that a University education was an integral part of one's education combined, of course, with a thorough Jewish education. When we emigrated to the United States in 1939, I was enrolled in a Yiddish-speaking, Eastern European style Yeshiva in Brooklyn. Being himself of Eastern European origin, my father was convinced that I would receive the best possible Talmudic education in such an institution. My Talmudic education continued at Yeshiva University where I studied for seven years with Rabbi Joseph Soloveitchik, one of the leading Talmudists of the postwar era. Concurrently, first at the City College of New York and then at Columbia University, I was studying philosophy.

My interest in philosophy developed rather early—at about the age of sixteen. As an undergraduate in a philosophy of religion course, I was introduced to Søren Kierkegaard and while at first I had great difficulty in making out what he was driving at (the first book I read was *Either/Or*, whose pseudonyms confused me no end), I knew from the beginning that here was someone of decisive importance to me. The fact that I wrote my doctoral dissertation on Kierkegaard and Heidegger[1] is an indication of the impact

---

1. *Kierkegaard and Heidegger: The Ontology of Existence* (New York: Humanities Press, 1954, 1969).

Kierkegaard and existentialism had on me. Through Kierkegaard I was drawn into Christian theology.

As I look back at it now, I find it difficult to disentangle the two strands: Kierkegaard and Christian theology. The two, of course, are very closely interwoven in Kierkegaard. At the same time, I suppose, one can be a sort of Kierkegaardian without being a Christian. But I never separated the two. To me, Kierkegaard was a Christian theologian and I dealt with him as such.

Christian theology attracted me because it combined my two most important interests: religion and philosophy. That is not to say that this combination is unknown in Judaism. There are quite a few Jewish figures who combine the two (e.g., Saadia and Maimonides) but the enterprise, as such, is not at the center of Judaism. The explication of the Torah with special emphasis on its legal portions is at the center while, for me, the basic religious questions of Judaism were most important. I also quickly learned to distinguish between philosophy of religion and theology. The former dealt with general problems of God and creation rather than with the specific content of revelation. Theology, as the relatively systematic formulation of the content of faith, was a largely Christian enterprise.

Before turning specifically to Barth, I must ask myself what significance the figure of Jesus of Nazareth had for me then. Was he not an insurmountable barrier for a believing Jew? That he was a barrier cannot be denied. But he was not an insurmountable barrier. The issue to me was faith in God, and it did not, and does not, seem to me ultimately important whether God did or did not somehow inhabit the body of Jesus of Nazareth. Whenever Christians spoke about Christ, I read it as referring to God and found that then everything made a great deal of sense. I did not for a moment doubt that the deification of Jesus was a mistake, even a serious mistake. But it was not a fatal mistake.

My dissertation was finished in the spring of 1952 and after that I began broadening my knowledge both of contemporary continental philosophy and theology. I focused particulary on Husserl, whom I should have known better while writing my dissertation. While I read a number of Christian theologians such as Tillich and Bultmann, it was Barth who attracted me more and more. Until I got very much involved with Barth, Kierkegaard had been my hero. For me, he had made faith possible in the twentieth century by delineating the realm of faith as an autonomous domain that was not the pale reflection of reason without the evidence. I found the lesson of this insight missing in both Bultmann and Tillich. Bultmann was so engrossed in the literary-historical interpretation of the New Testament that the question of what he believed receded into the background. For both Bultmann and Tillich, the influence of Heidegger had seriously undermined the centrality of the Bible as the real source of their thought. Bultmann read the New Testament through the spectacles of a Heideggerian analysis of human being while Tillich went beyond this and appropriated Heidegger's obsession with being without realizing how problematic this was for Christian faith.

At first, I found the autobiographical method lacking in Barth. When Kierkegaard wrote about Christianity, he wrote about his inner life, the vicissitudes of his personal and spiritual autobiography. This was not the case with Barth. Nevertheless, I sensed a genuine atmosphere of faith in his thought. Above all, the historical record was never pursued for its own sake. After surveying masterfully that record with respect to any given question, Barth always returns to the really important question: based on this history, what can we believe today? Above all, what drew me to Barth was that the power of the biblical word remained fully alive in his thought. It was the source of his energy, that which drove the whole vast enterprise and to which he was willing to subordinate his inclinations.

Nowhere was this more clear than in his treatment of Israel. Scandalous as this must seem to the natural human mind, the Hebrew Bible places the history and destiny of the Jewish people into the very center of God's interaction with humanity. Very few Christian theologians can cope with this fact. Most of them just ignore it or, when they must face up to it, they relegate it to the pre-Christian stage of the history of Israel, surpassed by the universalism of the church. This is not possible for Barth because the bias for the general, the universal, the nonspecific is absent in his thought. The result is that, to an unusual extent, the encounter with Israel remains alive in his thought. That is not to say that this encounter is unproblematic (I have detailed some of the problems elsewhere); in spite of the problems, the seriousness with which Barth takes the election of Israel and the specificity with which this election is carried over to the Jewish people of today is unique in the pages of Christian theology.

When I ask myself whether it was Kierkegaard or Barth who had the more decisive influence on my development, I cannot give an unequivocal answer. Kierkegaard was certainly the more powerful influence, if only because I read him at a more impressionable age.

Barth lacks the autobiographical authenticity of Kierkegaard, the interweaving of life and thought that has always seemed to me the most honest approach since it is, in fact, what we all do, except that most of us work rather hard at hiding it. On the other hand, the more I worked with Barth, the more his yielding to the authority of the Bible impressed me. The turmoils of our lives are, after all, not Scripture. Kierkegaard's break with Regina is not part of God's revelation to Israel or the Church. So I am not as convinced as I used to be that it is absolutely essential to put one's life at the center of one's theology. At the same time, I cannot give up the conviction that the life of the theologian does have a decisive influence on his thought. Barth's encounter with Nazism is an example of such influence. In short, this question requires further thought.

With respect to the substance of Barth's thought, curiously enough it is his recognition of Israel's sinfulness that has influenced me very much. This is curious because Israel's sinfulness is a prominent theme in almost all of Christian theology. Why, then, did Barth's expression of this insight have particular meaning for me? I can speculate that it is his generally positive view of Israel that made the difference. The discovery of Israel's sinfulness is one thing when it comes from a Christian theologian who believes that Israel has been superseded by the church and that Israel's sorrows are the result of its obstinacy. It is something entirely different when it comes from a Christian theologian with roots in Judaism as deep as those of Barth. Coming from such a source, the charge had to be investigated carefully.

Barth is right, of course. The history of Israel is a history of almost continuous rebellion. Most Jews do not like to talk about this. Nevertheless, it is true because the Bible says so and because we can see it with our eyes. And in spite of this, God loves the Jewish people in a special way. This is the triumph of God's grace over the obduracy of the human being. This grace so envelops Israel that it sees itself loved and saved by God, in spite of all its sufferings. It is thus easy for Israel to lose sight of the sorry record it has made in its relation with God. While traditional Judaism had no difficulty in acknowledging this, post-holocaust Judaism simply could not accept the commensurability of the punishment with the crime. Nevertheless, it would be folly to overlook the record of rebellion in the history of the people chosen by God for his special service.

At the same time, I have often wondered why Christians can only see the disobedience of Israel and never its faithfulness. Does not

God say to Israel (Jer. 2:2): "I remember for you the affection of your youth, the love of your espousals, how you went after me in the wilderness, in a land that was not sown"? The record of disobedience is there. But so is the faithfulness, the trust in God, the willingness to stake everything on the promise. Why do Christians, and why did Barth, find it so easy to overlook the positive side of Israel's response and focus exclusively on the disobedience?

In a 1967 letter, Barth wrote:

> I am decidedly not a philosemite, in that in personal encounters with living Jews (even Jewish Christians) I have always, so long as I can remember, had to suppress a totally irrational aversion, naturally suppressing it at once on the basis of all my presuppositions, and concealing it totally in my statements, yet still having to suppress and conceal it. Pfui! is all I can say to this in some sense allergic reaction of mine. But this is how it was and is. A good thing that this reprehensible instinct is totally alien to my sons and other better people than myself. . . . But it could have had a retrogressive effect on my doctrine of Israel.[2]

He·e is an honest admission by a great Christian theologian—perhaɟ s the greatest since Luther and Calvin—that he has an irrational dislike of Jews. One does not know whether to admire the man's courage for making the admission or to hold him in contempt for having the prejudice. And we must remember that the man who makes this admission had earlier written:

> Without any doubt the Jews are to this very day the chosen people of God in the same sense as they have been so from the beginning, according to the Old and New Testaments. They have the promise of God; and if we Christians from among the Gentiles have it too, then it is only as those chosen with them; as guests in their house, as new wood grafted onto their old tree.[3]

And again:

> For it is incontestable that this people as such is the people of God: the people with whom God has dealt in His grace and in His wrath; in the midst of whom He has blessed and judged, enlightened and hardened, accepted and rejected; whose cause either way He has made His own,

---

2. *Karl Barth Letters: 1961–1968*, ed. Jürgen Fangmeier and Hinrich Stoevesandt, trans. and ed. Geoffrey W. Bromiley (Grand Rapids: Eerdmans, 1981), p. 262.
3. Karl Barth, "The Jewish Problem and the Christian Answer" in *Against the Stream* (London: SCM Press, 1954), p. 200.

and has not ceased to make His own, and will not cease to make His own. They are all of them by nature sanctified by Him, sanctified as ancestors and kinsmen of the Holy One in Israel, in a sense that Gentiles are not by nature, not even the best of Gentiles, not even the Gentile Christians, not even the best of Gentile Christians, in spite of their membership of the Church, in spite of the fact that they too are now sanctified by the Holy One of Israel and have become Israel.[4]

How can a human being combine this theology of the Jewish people with a "totally irrational aversion" and an "allergic reaction" to this same people? One can only speculate about the feelings of Christians less honest than Barth, who do not share Barth's theology of the Jewish people.

On a sunny morning in August 1966 I visited Barth in his modest home on the Bruderholzallee in Basel. He had been told that I was a "Jewish Barthian," and this amused him no end. We spoke about various things and at one point he said: "You Jews have the promise but not the fulfillment; we Christians have both promise and fulfillment." Influenced by the banking atmosphere of Basel, I replied: "With human promises, one can have the promise but not the fulfillment. The one who promises can die, or change his mind, or not fulfill his promise for any number of reasons. But a promise of God is like money in the bank. If we have his promise, we have its fulfillment and if we do not have the fulfillment we do not have the promise." There was a period of silence and then he said: "You know, I never thought of it that way." I will never forget that meeting.

One of these years I will start rereading the *Church Dogmatics*. I am sure I will profit from it again.

4. Karl Barth, *Church Dogmatics*, II/2, 287.

Assessing Barth for Apologetics

Clark H. Pinnock

I was not immediately aware whether or in what manner Barth had changed my mind. I would have found it much easier to say how glad I am he changed his own mind. I am thankful that he abandoned religious liberalism first and then the radical dialectical theology later on. I would like to say how I welcome him warmly into the ranks of evangelical theologians, joining them in the defense of the gospel, and in the repudiation of the great apostasy from the classical paradigm. For to me, Barth is no new modernist, but rather a new ally in the orthodox tradition.

But I have been asked how Barth changed my mind, not his. And in answer to this more difficult question I would dwell upon an unexpected and surprising point. Barth has enriched my thinking by suggesting to me how one might improve the apologetic defense of Christianity in the modern world. Now we all know that Barth would not have wanted or intended to improve classical apologetics. He wanted to see it abolished, not improved. But he is dead and gone now and cannot prevent me from making the point I am going to make. Barth's great insistence upon the objectivity and concrete character of divine revelation can in fact be recycled and made to serve the apologetic defense of the faith.

I have always felt that Barth's emphasis here was theologically right and apologetically wrong. He was entirely right to insist that God reveals himself and sets his own terms for the divine-human encounter. He was right to focus our attention upon the Christological project as the high point in God's redemptive revelation. But I have always felt uncomfortable because of the fideistic overtones that his presentation conveys. I am convinced that Barth is a voluntarist in the matter of Christianity. The gospel has to be accepted or rejected by an act of the will (faith), and nothing can be said to justify the truth claims it makes by way of standard apologetic reasoning. Therefore it seems to me that Barth sees as essentially arbitrary the decision to accept Christianity as true over against another system of truth. Revelation is its own proof, and faith authenticates itself.

Having read Barth (correctly, I believe) in this way, I have always felt it necessary to turn away from him and pursue a more classical approach to religious knowledge. Believing as I do that Christianity is objectively true, I felt it imperative to recognize ways to test its claims for their truth value. There must be evidence independent of us as subjects that can help us to decide about ultimate issues. This decision is too important to be a mere voluntary one.

But it has occurred to me of late that there is a different light in which to view Barth's emphasis. I refer to his great stress upon the objective reality of divine revelation. The point first surfaced in his Anselm book. The knowledge of God is not just a possibility, Barth insists; it is a reality. God has revealed himself as gracious—what is actual must be possible. We do not have to discuss the matter in abstraction, he says, when it is a powerful reality already. From this point on Barth determined never to explore the possibility of revelation, but to proceed from its actuality, on the basis of its givenness. God in the midst of the burning bush does not invite us to a discussion but calls on us to repent and believe. I interpret Barth to be intending us to recognize revelation as a power-encounter. It does not need intellectual preparations and supports because it sweeps away everything in its path. As Paul said, the gospel is the power of God unto salvation (Rom. 1:16). It is not primarily a system of thought to be argued about but a transforming reality. One does not ask about the validity of sense perception when a flood of water is sweeping toward us. One moves and checks for mistakes later. If we think a time-bomb is about to explode, we do not discuss the properties of explosions. We evacuate the building. What Barth, I think, is calling attention to is the sheer reality of God's redemptive power that is even now challenging all the powers of this age.

If this is close to what Barth is driving at, then his antipathy to classical apologetics can be viewed in terms other than fideism. God's power to save has been released and therefore what the unbeliever needs is to be exposed to that saving power. What one needs more than a book of apologetics is contact with a Spirit-filled community that is a vehicle of the newness Jesus brought into the world. God is now changing the world, and this is the credentials of the gospel. If Christianity is true, it will prove to be true and unbelieving resistance to it will collapse. If it is not true in this power-encounter sense, no amount of learned apologetics can accomplish anything.

As one who celebrates the reality of Pentecost, I identify with Barth's point enthusiastically. The truth of the gospel is most certainly verified by reason of its ability to save and to deliver enslaved and hell-bound sinners. But I suspect Barth would not want to add this verification to the other points of verification housed in the arsenal of classical apologetics. I think he would want to say that it provides evidence only to the eyes of faith and that it cannot be, as it were, publicly accessible evidence to be employed like other pieces of promising evidence on behalf of the truth of the gospel. But I would want to ask, why not? Surely the fact that revelation is objective in the Incarnation and the resurrection, as Barth certainly insists, means that they are truth claims that can be examined in historical ways and commended to anyone precisely on the basis of their factuality. I cannot understand why Barth would insist on the objectivity of the resurrection, for example, and then leave it hanging in midair as if it had no solid evidences on the side of believing it. And surely the fact that millions of persons have testified to the quiet presence as well as the irruptive dynamic of God's reality in their lives is objective evidence of a compelling kind that speaks on behalf of the truth of Christian theism. I cannot understand why Barth would testify so vividly to the concreteness of revelation in the life of contemporary humans and then walk away from it, leaving it completely unexploited apologetically.

How has Barth changed my mind? His emphasis on the concrete actuality of revelation is obviously biblical and evangelical and begs to be given a nobler place in our apologetic efforts than it has been given. Though I encounter opposition from Barth himself in drawing out this point and receive little encouragement from classical apologists themselves, who often appear lacking in the sphere of the Holy Spirit, I press on to insist that Barth can help us forge a more balanced apologetic than is usual, an apologetic that employs both wisdom and power. Classical apologetics has emphasized wisdom, that is, the human gift of thinking things through so warmly recommended to us in the Book of Proverbs. There is a great promise in wisdom because it means that faith is nonarbitrary. There are reasons for faith and one can enter into faith intelligently. And now Barth comes along and emphasizes power, that is, the outpouring of the Spirit in the gospel. He points to the fact that God did not wait to be discovered by the philosophers, but established his own reality and identity by revealing himself. But power and wisdom are not in contradiction. We proclaim the action of God in Jesus Christ and are prepared to give a reason for the hope that is in us. Like Barth we proclaim what God has done, and unlike Barth we are ready to defend what we proclaim. And that defense includes the power about which Barth speaks, but also the historical evidence backing up the Incarnation claim and the metaphysical arguments commending the validity of theism. Barth helps me see the importance of the charismatic dimension in Christian apologetics and thus improves the quality of classical apologetics without intending to do so. I wonder if Barth, given his well-known sense of humor, is even now chuckling at this suggestion, or, even better, scratching his head and wondering whether he should not have changed his mind on this matter also!

Karl Barth: How His Mind Kept Changing

John H. Yoder

There would be room for intensive study of the phases through which the appropriation of Karl Barth in America passed, leading to one discrepancy after another between what he was doing at the time and how he was being read. The existentialistic tone of the *Romans* commentary was being responded to in America in the 1930s as if Barth were against systematic thought, whereas by then he had begun the most ambitious systematic *summa* of the century. The apparent occasionalism with which ethics was introduced in *Church Dogmatics* II/2 was being read in America as a rejection of all possible general statements about right behavior and as skepticism about whether in the field of ethics we can say anything specific about the shape of the will of God, while in Basel Barth had begun lecturing with great detail about the casuistry of respect for life. In 1957 Reinhold Niebuhr could ask, "Why is Barth silent about Hungary?" while Barth, in conversation with his old friend Josef Hromadka, had been writing and lecturing for a decade about the new challenge living under Marxist governments posed, in light of the need to distinguish the gospel not only from official unbelief but also from the established posture of religion farther west.

Students went from North America to Basel to study "theology as such," in the sense in which "neo-orthodoxy" had come to stand for the restored dignity of the theological task as heir to the Reformation. They found Barth in his lectures and seminars conversing with Sartre about nothingness or with Thomas about angels.

It is fitting that we here should seek to reach back behind the delayed American appropriation in order to reconstruct on its own an outline of how what was developing would have looked from within its own dynamic, correcting for the need of transatlantic quests to find resources for their own agenda.

Such a rereading has been facilitated by the progress of the Barth archives in publishing his early correspondence. It has been moti-

vated for some by their concern for Barth's early socialism, for some
by the search for the beginnings of sensitivity to the evil of anti-
Judaism, for still others by their concern for ecclesiology or the
theory of preaching. The revision, in other words, has also had its
own apologetic or corrective concerns. Barth would not have had it
otherwise. Nonetheless it is fitting that beyond our own interests in
the uses of the heritage, we should seek ways to discern behind all the
apologetic skirmishes whether there was any architectonic design
implicit in the way the entire corpus of Barthian thought grew.

There is nothing fresh about looking at the direction implicit in
the internal outline of the *Dogmatics.* The table of contents of each
volume testified to Barth's combination of playfulness and elegance;
but can we say about the theological import of Barth's entire production, including the political involvement and the correspondence,
that it was moving in a particular direction?

For most of those American Christian thinkers who remember
having watched it happening, what Karl Barth came to represent in
the drama of changing theology in the middle of our century was
primarily the ambitious and in some ways successful attempt to
construct a *summa,* restoring the notion of systematic theology as a
constructive discipline, reaching from Scripture through history to
the present in a thoroughly coherent and conclusive system. For such
people, to call Barth "neo-orthodox" meant then that he restored,
for a generation who had lost faith in that possibility, a vision of the
dignity of the theological task, and of the continuing usefulness of
the classical literary heritage as a resource for those who discharged
that task.

A subsegment of this first context is the concern of some to find in
the overarching systematic vision of Barth some specific new focus
that one could hold to be especially promising or especially threatening, such as "the triumph of grace." He restored not only the dignity
of theology but also that of *systematic* theology: the discipline of
coherent structures moving from first principles through their logical
implications.

For another, smaller group of his readers, who continued to read
him as genuinely their own teacher, Karl Barth is the thinker who
rediscovered for his day and for ours a way of articulating the gospel
of Jesus Christ that makes it again truly good news, a preachable
message of salvation for a postliberal world in which before he came
along it had seemed there was no longer any credible good news.
These admirers see the term *neo-orthodox* as inappropriate, since it

groups Barth with a handful of his contemporaries who were doing other things and teaching other gospels. It is not indispensable, for these disciples, to know just at what point the renewed radicalness of Barth's vision of grace has to call for some social structure other than the one we have, or to issue in some social ethic other than those which preceded his ministry.

Both of the above visions are true. The truth of the second is nearer to the heart of the matter than the first. Yet there is a still more adequate way to understand what the Barthian renewal program was about. It should be no surprise that such an alternative interpretation should center not on where Barth came from, or how he first began to innovate, but on where he was going. The aptness of such a view would be confirmed rather than refuted by the recognition that he had not got there yet. His vision, like the *Church Dogmatics,* remains unfinished. Yet that directional characterization can find its validation in his theological and ecclesiastical trajectory, which the other two characterizations do not explain. From the outset Barth was clear about being on the move; all that needs to be done now is to identify his direction.

Those who in the 1930s attached the label "neo-orthodox" to Karl Barth (as to other contemporaries who differed importantly from him) were guided by their own perception of the lay of the land in Protestant theology at the time. They assumed a dominant classical debate between orthodoxy and liberalism. The former included commitment both to the foundations of the Protestant Reformation and to the authority of the Bible. The latter was characterized generally by a post-Enlightenment epistemological openness to doctrinal change and especially by critical perspectives on the Scriptures. When the lay of the land had been thus defined, it was not false to say that the "neo-orthodox" were going beyond the latter to a newly respectful, creative reappropriation of the former.

That was what made Barth initially most attractive to theologians and pastors in Reformed communities and theological schools in the Netherlands, Scotland, and North America. Not false, but not adequate. A phrase like "creative reappropriation of the values of the orthodox heritage" does not explain the differences that quite soon divided Barth from the other great figures (notably Brunner and the Niebuhrs), to whom the same characterization was (not falsely) applied by fad-watchers.

It is more important to seek to characterize Karl Barth strategically not by the way in which he did and did not continue the lines set by his heritage, but by where he was going, even though—by the nature of the case—such a reading of the implicit trajectory must be based on an unfinished story. I shall seek to identify those points at which Barth's incomplete pilgrimage can best be understood as being on the way to what Anglo-Saxon ecclesiological thinking calls the Free Church.

Barth's use of the Bible is that of the free churchman. He does not pick up the Scriptures again (reaching past the curtain of liberal relativizing) as validation for the corpus of orthodox dogma that claims to be its marrow or its equivalent. From his early statement that he was going to read Romans as if the author knew what he was saying, to the later appearance of long expository excurses in *Church Dogmatics,* the Bible functions as fount or fulcrum for a constantly renewed, nondogmatic critical, and recreative debate. This is the radical potential of the slogan *ecclesia reformata semper reformanda;* it is the point of Puritan John Robinson's "The Lord has much more light and truth to break forth from His holy Word." Creeds and compendia are respected but made relative.

Barth's appeal to the Bible is not that of a "presuppositionalist" claim to an a priori authority resident in an inspired text; it in fact eschews any claim to "higher ground" or general validity from which truth claims could be "validated." Such a renunciation of a higher claim is not sectarianism but modesty, freed from the need of self-accreditation. In this respect Barth is not precritical but postmodern.

Barth's modulation of socialism moves toward that of the free churchman. His socialist commitment as a young pastor, unionizing workers and writing disrespectful open letters to factory owners, showed little originality. Without ever disavowing the socialist analysis of what is wrong with Western industrial society, or the dialectical reading of how being precedes consciousness, his move from the pastorate to the university, his criticism of programmatic political socialism as also a form of worldly humanism, and his sitting loose to contemporary party controversies mean—although this was not said programmatically then—that the locus of economic reformation is not in political economy but in Christology.

Barth's ecclesiology is most original at the point where the concrete community of believers begins to be able to foster a critical perspective on the Constantinian form of churchliness as the theological dimension of an entire society. Critical attention to his *Christengemeinde und Bürgergemeinde* has questioned the uneven and whimsical use Barth makes of the notion of analogy, whereby the faith language of the believing community might be so transposed as to converse in the civil community. What matters, however, is the *prior* axiom, unprecedented in the thought of his teachers and contemporaries, whether orthodox or liberal, that there are two quite distinct principles of community, *so that* there must be different structures of community, *so that* there must be different moral and legal languages. The value of *Christengemeinde und Bürgergemeinde* is not the exploratory way the notion of analogy is played out, but the specific identity of the community of Christians that makes one ask the questions which that notion seeks to answer.

What *Christengemeinde und Bürgergemeinde* intimates, *Church Dogmatics* IV/2 spells out (The Order of the Community, esp. pp. 719ff.: True Church order is exemplary order). The ordered structure of human togetherness is not univocal. There is the order of believing community, an order of servanthood and doxology. It is not derived from the shape of the civil order, as for Bullinger, Erastus, or Luther, or for the sociologists' understanding of "religion"; the derivation goes the other way. But it really does go the other way; the order enabled by the gospel is the paradigm for what God intends for all humankind.

Barth's free church sympathies found concrete expression as well when in his last years he picked up conversation with Zinzendorf and with contemporary Moravians and Mennonites.

German Protestant usage has long been divided between Pietists and Baptists who used the term *Gemeinde* to speak of the people of God, and those Catholic and magisterial Protestant thinkers who used *Kirche*. Both can be used to render *ekklesia*. *Gemeinde* means more the gathered people, *Kirche* means first the polity. The thrust of Barth's preference for *Gemeinde* is largely lost in the English translation. Rendering *Gemeinde* as "congregation" only comes through in English when it means the *local* gathering.

Should any have failed to note this free church tendency as general teaching in Barth's ecclesiology, none can miss his evident movement with regard to baptism. In the 1930s infant baptism was challenged from the perspective of the Reformed view of the sacraments. Sacraments signify, according to Zwingli and Calvin. How then can an infant be the recipient of signifying? The mature rejection of paedobaptism in Vol. IV moves deeper to see baptism as the confessional act constituting a visible countercultural community, distinct by its very nature from the rest of the world (or its religions), which infant baptism tends to sanctify.

What we saw above with regard to socialism applies as well to Barth's pacifism; it is transformed along his path from prophetic liberalism in 1914 to nuclear pacifism in the 1950s. He first had to set aside the socialist/internationalist pacifism of 1914 (rendered further unpalatable by his personal rift with Leonhard Ragaz) and any root-age of antimilitarism in legalism, historical optimism, or social irresponsibility before he could renew his own critique of the traditional acceptance of war. His critique was dual. In the nuclear pacifism of the *Kirchliche Bruderschaften* in 1958 he followed Barmen's Article V in an affirmation, critical and courageous but not theologically original, of the *limited* mandate of the state, from which is derived a negative use of Just War categories. Deeper, because Christological, is Barth's access to pacifism under the rubric of sanctification. The approach of "The Holy One and the Holy Ones" marked the maturing of a shift from a Christology where the Jesus of the chapters on Nicea and Chalcedon was little more than a cipher for the concept of revelation, to the human figure of the evangelical accounts. If discipleship is to be ethical rather than only pietistic, the One we follow must be known in his humanness. Therefore it is no surprise that the *prima facie* pacifist import of sanctification goes beyond Bonhoeffer both formally and substantively.

The free church position is intrinsically unfinished. Barth's path from mainline to radical churchmanship is unfinished not only because the *Church Dogmatics* remained a torso, and not only because at some points (his pacifism being only "practical," his rejecting "rebaptism") he had a cultural stake in not seeming to join the sectarians (though that is a good reason too). The freedom of the church is a command and a hope, not the property of Baptists. Nonetheless there is no other characterization of the *ductus* of his growth. He is not rehabilitating orthodoxy or establishment. Though he renews conversation with Schleiermacher and with Rome, it is not with a view to rehabilitating their priorities. Since IV/2 there is no refuting his commitment to the free church vision.

Barth and the Barthians: A Critical Appraisal

John B. Cobb, Jr.

It would be hard to doubt that Barth is the greatest theologian of our century. He made the greatest impact on the history of the discipline. He did so by the power and richness of his thought and scholarship. Probably his impact on the institutional life of the church was also greater than that of any other person.

Much of what he did can be applauded by Christians of all persuasions. He brought the Bible in its own integrity into the contemporary discussion, making relative the power of the idealist tradition to control the way it was read and interpreted. He shifted attention from our ideas of God to God and God's actual work in the world. He gave a generation of preachers the courage to proclaim the gospel without apology or embarrassment. He gave Christians in Germany a place to stand firm against the seduction of Nazism, meanwhile helping Christians in other countries such as Japan to understand their situation in politically difficult times. He undercut in principle the *arrogance* of Christendom in its attitude toward "other religions." He reduced, if he did not obliterate, the theological grounds for anti-Judaism. He understood that his teachings were shaped in part by his time and circumstances and encouraged others to seek an analogous faithfulness to God's Word in their times and circumstances, explicitly opposing the formation of a specific school of thought. He countered, in some measure, the long-term trend toward privatization and marginalization of Christian thought. For a generation and more he provided a mode of theology to which many from both the theological left and the theological right could subscribe, thus greatly strengthening the cause of ecumenicity.

From my perspective, he also made mistakes for which the price has been high. His treatment of fellow theologians was such as to encourage the public image of theology as a scene of competition. There was no need for him to misrepresent such colleagues as Emil Brunner and Reinhold Niebuhr and to attack them so brutally. It seemed that whereas he opposed a Barthian school he also opposed every approach to Christian understanding that differed from his own. Although his own did provide a basis for much ecumenical work, in the academic world it became, inevitably, just one theology alongside others. By representing these others as antithetical, he promoted, contrary to his intention, an attitude of theological relativism. Whereas the readers of Brunner and Niebuhr sense that they can learn from both theologians as well as from Barth, the reader of Barth concludes that one must choose. Barth is, despite his avowed opposition to it, partly responsible for Barthianism and for the relativistic spirit spawned in reaction by the plurality of "isms."

My criticism is motivated in part by my sense of indebtedness to Niebuhr for his illumination of the human condition and his display of the relevance of the biblical perspective to the understanding of contemporary history. It is affected also by my sense of kinship with Brunner in his call for Christian natural theology and a Christian critique of, and contribution to, all the disciplines. But my point here is to say that faithfulness to the Word need not generate the harsh rejections characteristic of Barth and that a style of openness to the contributions of others would have encouraged shared work among colleagues rather than party spirit. It might also have avoided the violent swing of the pendulum in the 1960s.

I refer, of course, to the "radical theology" and the "death of God theology" that burst upon the scene around 1965. They revitalized the public discussion of theology. But they did so in a primarily negative way and drove a wedge between theology and the church. The new situation directed the church away from theology for practical guidance. It may seem odd to blame Barth for this movement, or explosion of movements, but the connection is factually as well as theoretically apparent.

The connection was made most explicit by Paul Van Buren, one of the first North Americans to complete graduate studies under Barth's guidance at Basel. In *The Secular Meaning of the Gospel* he argued that we must translate theological language into secular language. The reason? Barth had shown that all natural theology must be rejected. Linguistic analysis shows that without a natural theology all language must be about the world. Barth's total rejection of Brunner's proposal bore its fruit!

Lest one suppose that Van Buren's argument was arbitrary, consider the situation. Barth talked extensively about God. But if we ask Barth what he means by "God," the only answers we can get are in the language and thought-forms of the Bible. Barth systematically opposes any translation of these forms into those of our time or even any effort to build a bridge between these worlds. He writes for those who by faith already stand within the biblical thought world. But this means that for actual human beings, inevitably shaped in most of their thinking by modern thought, "God" is a meaningless word. If it is to become meaningful, it must be translated into our language. But Barth forbids us to use our language to refer beyond the world. Hence "God" must refer to our world or be completely meaningless. Van Buren chose the former option.

Most advocates of radical or atheistic theology did not reason explicitly in this way, but they and their followers reflected this kind of logic nonetheless. William Hamilton and Thomas Altizer also acknowledged Barth as their teacher. On Barthian terms one must order one's life around a purported reality with which contemporary thought makes no contact, or else one must deny any transcendent God altogether. Barth's influence excluded for many any other course. Thomists, Tillichians, Niebuhrians, and we process theologians watched this reversal with keen interest, but few of us participated. We did not experience the alternatives in this way.

I have explained already my deepest reason for having always viewed Barth's thought with some detachment. Interesting and impressive it certainly was, but it was also, for me, incredible in the strict sense. Barth taught that theology was the critical articulation of the church's belief—it was not intended to explain the faith or to make it credible to unbelievers. In my personal crisis of faith I needed just what he excluded. The images by which I had thought of God had collapsed because they did not fit with the world into which I was plunged by my university experience. Barth's images were of no use. So I was compelled to choose between unbelief and natural theology—a Christian natural theology. I chose then, and choose now, this option. Indeed, the events of the sixties confirmed my suspicion that in fact my personal needs were not idiosyncratic but reflective of a widespread need of the church in the modern world.

There are those today who say Barth has been misunderstood, that he was not as opposed as I have suggested to responding to authentic doubt. Perhaps they are correct. But the question is not of great importance. Barth as a powerful factor in the public world was perceived in this way and Barthians followed what they saw in Barth in treating people like me with suspicion and condescension. If now our criticisms seem unfair, understand that they reflect the cumulative pain of exclusion and humiliation that we felt from a generally Barthian ecumenical consensus. We can only hope that now that that consensus has faded and we are allowed to enter and partly to shape the establishment, we will remember the importance of a spirit of openness and inclusiveness in dealing with those who find our solutions just as incredible as we found Barth's and who struggle for other avenues to faith.

I have spoken of remaining an observer of radical and atheistic theology seen as a logical reversal of Barth's formulations and of his rejection of other theological approaches. There was another movement, or family of movements, during the same period, also arising among Barthians, to which I have responded in a quite different way. Barth's imaging of God suggested a vertical transcendence. In the 1960s this was changed for many of those influenced by Barth into a horizontal transcendence, the transcendence of the future. Even Altizer could be read this way. Pannenberg, Moltmann, and several Latin American theologians have made this move explicit. I have not found this conceptually satisfactory either. All the formulations are for me either unconvincing or too vague to judge. But this move has opened up a range of reflection and action to history, and therefore to justice, that I find admirable, illuminating, and compelling. If I "blame" Barth for "the death of God," I must give him some credit for black, liberation, and political theology as well as for the penetrating insights of Pannenberg's theology of history and overview of the sciences.

The Barthian background of these developments showed itself initially in a continuing suspicion of "natural theology," including Christian natural theology. The reasons, however, were different. The objection now was more toward what was supposed to be a "cosmic" and therefore nonhistorical approach than toward the general effort to establish critical continuities between contemporary conceptualities and faith. Pannenberg, especially, quickly moved to much more nuanced and insightful criticism as a genuine conversation-partner. Others have come more slowly to see that a Christian natural theology, even when related to natural sciences, need not cut against the concern for history and justice. The possibility of fruitful dialogue and even collaboration arises at last. Perhaps in a shared concern for a stricken humanity, the heirs of Barth and the heirs of those who could not follow him can at last come together in dialogue and mutual support!

Such flowing together of disparate streams is not yet accomplished. It requires a confession on the part of those, like myself, for whom natural theology is essential, that in our theological writings we long neglected the concern for justice, so central to the new post-Barthian developments. The reason was, I think, that our defensiveness in relation to the Barthian consensus led us to abandon our heritage in the social gospel and to concentrate our energies elsewhere. But if these concerns are truly required by our understanding of God and the world, we must show and embody them, not merely apologize. Until that happens, suspicion of us will be justified. We have made a good beginning, but more is needed.

On the other side, we detect limitations and hindrances that are the remaining legacy of Barth, or of the larger tradition of which Barth was part. This has to do especially with the natural world. I praised Barth at the outset for breaking out of the limitations of the Kantian tradition in which so often the topic of theological discussion is the concept of God rather than God. Barth spoke undeniably of the biblical God. But Barth did not successfully overcome the limitation, on the other side, to the *concept* of nature. Whatever his intention, for Barthians generally, "nature" remained bound to the human perception of the human environment. The independent actuality of natural events and their importance for human destiny remained excluded from theological discourse. What is happening to the natural world in terms of desertification, the poisoning of air, soil, and water, the disappearance of forests, the melting of the polar ice, the rapid extinction of species, the loss of topsoil, the depletion of irreplaceable resources, and the decrease of the ozone layer—all this remains either outside of theology or at its periphery as one of the minor questions to be mentioned occasionally. For those who subscribe to a Christian natural theology, or at least for those who fashion such a theology along lines like mine, a different mindset seems appropriate—one that locates human history radically within the history of the biosphere. On the side of the post-Barthians, a beginning has been made. Both Pannenberg and Moltmann are sensitive to "environmental issues," as are some liberation theologians. Hence no wall prevents communication.

Indeed, there are those who are both liberation theologians and process theologians. Perhaps a generation is appearing to which such labels will be superfluous. They will genuinely seek to bring the whole gospel to the whole world of thought and suffering life. They will devote their energies not to putting one another down or to mutual exclusion but to a shared effort to respond appropriately to the enormous challenge posed by contemporary intellectual life to Christian belief as well as, and together with, responding to injustice, to unsustainability, and to the threat of nuclear annihilation.

My hope in this respect is strengthened by events already transpiring. Of several people I could mention, I select just one—Michael Welker. A leading student of Jürgen Moltmann, he was encouraged by his mentor to write his *Habilitationschrift* on Whitehead and process theology. He did so—critically, of course, but also with remarkable appreciation. He has appropriated much from this mode and maintains a friendly and actively supportive relationship to it. He has not, of course, cut himself off from the rich theological tradition in which he stands. As a young professor at Tübingen he unites these streams of thought creatively in his own person.

So what of Barth? That I could not follow him does not mean I cannot admire him or appreciate much of his legacy. That appreciation can best be shown today, not by becoming Barthians, but by responding as creatively to our situation, as we understand it, as he did to his, as he understood it.

Ad Majorem Dei Gloriam

Geoffrey Wainwright

The first of Karl Barth's works to exercise a specific influence on me was one of those little writings that he did so well. Soon after leaving theological college in 1964 I was asked to contribute a short book on *Christian Initiation* to a series of ecumenical studies published by Lutterworth in Britain and by John Knox in the United States. Hitherto I had had few problems with the baptism of infants. In scouting the literature I came across Barth's 1943 lecture to Swiss theological students, translated by the English Baptist Ernest Payne under the title *The Teaching of the Church Regarding Baptism*. What a shock to find such an unimpeachable proponent of prevenient grace expressing his *preference* for baptism upon personal profession of faith! I eventually came around to that position myself, though I had not quite gotten there in my first book. I still hold that the *primary* agent in baptism for the glorifying of God and the upbuilding of the church is Christ himself ("Christus est qui baptizat"), *and* that there is properly a *second* agent: the baptized person becomes an active partner in the saving covenant in pledging grateful allegiance to the service of the Deliverer. I was never convinced, however, by Barth's restriction of the divine function in baptism to a cognitive one over against a causative or generative one. That was the distinction which finally allowed him, in a fragment of *Church Dogmatics* IV/4, to separate Spirit-baptism from water-baptism in such a way as to reduce the latter to a merely human acknowledgment. I judge it quite possible, indeed exegetically requisite, to hold firmly to the sacraments as "means of grace" while considering professing believers to be their proper subjects. It is feasible to give a theological account of this in accordance with a theory of communicative signs.

More generally, Karl Barth early confirmed me in the content and direction of the Christian faith as I had come to experience it in an elementary and only inchoately reflective way; and this confirmation gradually helped me to adopt a theological perspective and method that is consonant with Barth, even if it is not the only one that could be drawn from him. Barth had an overriding concern for the glory of

God, its manifestation and proclamation: within my limitations I have turned to doxology for motive and material. Already in the seventeenth and eighteenth of his Gifford Lectures of 1937-38, *The Knowledge of God and the Service of God According to the Teaching of the Reformation,* Barth presented the liturgical assembly as the "concrete center" of the church's life: "The church service is the most important, momentous and majestic thing which can possibly take place on earth, because its primary content is not the work of man but the work of the Holy Spirit and consequently the work of faith" (p. 198). By the proclamation and faithful hearing of the Word the church is led back to her beginnings in baptism and forward to her destiny in the Lord's Supper. By her worshipful obedience the church glorifies God's name in her own midst and in the world, thus fulfilling the human vocation (as the fourth lecture stated it) of rendering God glory by reflection.

Unfortunately, in the *Church Dogmatics* the places are all too rare in which Barth develops his theology of worship. An example is found in IV/2, 695-710: "It is only as the (Christian) community has its distinct center in its worship that it can and will stand out clearly from the world. But this is necessary as in its history there is to be a representation of the particular history of its Head, an attestation of Jesus Christ" (p. 697; cf. also pp. 638-41). And again in IV/3, 883-84:

> Where else in the world does it take place that God is thanked for the love with which He has turned to the world and asked that He will turn to it again with this love? . . . It is the (Christian) community which with its prayer no less than its praise can act representatively for the world, going on before and introducing as a witness this fact, this obvious likeness, of reconciliation, the covenant and fellowship between God and man. (see also pp. 865-66)

Appeal to the liturgical life of the church and its significative function would have strengthened Barth's argument in another small writing that early influenced me and that I still consider to set the right perspective for Christian engagement in social and political life. In *Christengemeinde und Bürgergemeinde* (1946), Barth argued that it is the church's responsibility to bear witness before the world to those values of God's kingdom which are known to faith and which it is the business of the civil community to mirror at least in an external, relative, and provisional way. That analogical relation between church, society, and kingdom underlies the liturgically more concrete theological ethics of my *Doxology.* Already in *Eucharist and Eschatology,* I argued that a properly ordered eucharist exemplifies justice because grateful people are all equally welcomed there by the merciful Lord into his table fellowship and all together share in the fruits of redemption and in the foretaste of the new heavens and the new earth in which right will prevail; it exemplifies peace, because reconciled people are there at peace with God and with one another; it exemplifies joy in the Holy Ghost, because the cup of blessing conveys to all who partake of it a taste of that sober intoxication which the Spirit gives. Having learned and experienced this in the paradigm of the eucharistic meal, the church is committed to an everyday witness in word and deed that will give the opportunity for all the material resources of creation and all occasions of human contact to become the medium of that communion with God and among human beings which is marked by justice, peace, and joy in the Holy Ghost, and in which the kingdom of God consists.

Barth himself was remarkably unconcrete in his liturgical vision. How the practical performance of worship might reflect a largely Barthian theology I learned more from Jean-Jacques von Allmen of Neuchâtel. Barth remained a prisoner of the liturgical insipidity of German-speaking Switzerland. He was gravely suspicious of the visual: the plastic arts are too "static," "fixed," whereas the congregation should be moving on "from one provisional Amen to another"; and even the best artists are "necessarily" either docetic, as in "the great Italians," or ebionite, as in Rembrandt (*CD* IV/3, 867-68). Thus the icon and with it the whole world of Eastern Orthodoxy were closed to him. Although Barth theoretically recognized the truncated character of a Sunday service without the Lord's Supper, one had the impression that he was in actuality quite well satisfied with a sermon surrounded by a couple of prayers and a couple of hymns. Even the organ could threaten the ministry of the *vox humana* (IV/3, 867), yet Barth did acknowledge the theological importance of congregational singing.

That was the nearest Barth ever came to Methodism. Although he took on a couple of Methodist doctoral students, he shared the continental European prejudice concerning the untheological character of Methodism. He will certainly be amused to find at least one chapter by a writer of that allegiance in this volume. As a twentieth-century Methodist, I am grateful for the way in which Barth revolutionized the Calvinist doctrine of predestination. From being categories that fixed persons from the start and forever, election and reprobation became a dialectical process that focused on Christ—the eternal Son and the inclusive head of a human race called to communion with God, redeemed after its fall, and having the gates of reconciliation open before it. That is a better background than Wesley found in contemporary Calvinism for his understanding of God's plan "to save man as man; to set life and death before him, and then persuade (not force) him to choose life."

As an ecumenist, I am grateful for Barth's increasing willingness, toward the end of his life, to take the Roman Catholic Church with ecclesial seriousness. The Second Vatican Council closed out Barth's theological life just as it opened up the beginning of mine. His movingly described visit "ad limina apostolorum" practically coincided with my own working in the libraries of Pontifical institutions on my doctoral dissertation. I am glad to have had the Catholic Church as more than a sparring partner throughout my career.

Never a pupil of Barth's, I met him only briefly in his later years. An astonishing vigor stayed with him. It must have fed into and from that massive confidence which allowed him to set up position and opposition and never leave one in doubt as to which side one was expected to stand on. The theological picture I paint is on a smaller scale and my colors are rather more muted. But I felt in touch with redemptive history—and even caught an indirect glimpse of God's glory—on that day in Lichfield, England, when, for ten pence because it was a "foreign book," I picked up after forty years a first edition of *Theologische Existenz heute!* For some of my students, the use of another fragment of *Church Dogmatics* IV/4 to teach the Lord's Prayer has had that effect also. And so:

> Come, let us join our friends above
> That have obtained the prize,
> And on the eagle wings of love
> To joys celestial rise;
> Let all the saints terrestrial sing,
> With those to glory gone;
> For all the servants of our King,
> In earth and heaven, are one.
> (Charles Wesley)

Contributors

Elizabeth Achtemeier	Visiting Professor of Bible and Homiletics Union Theological Seminary Richmond, Virginia
Christoph F. Barth	Emeritus Professor of Old Testament University of Mainz Federal Republic of West Germany
Markus Barth	Professor of New Testament University of Basel Basel, Switzerland
Hendrikus Berkhof	Professor of Theology Emeritus University of Leiden Leiden, The Netherlands
Donald G. Bloesch	Professor of Theology University of Dubuque Theological Seminary Dubuque, Iowa
Geoffrey W. Bromiley	Senior Professor of Church History and Historical Theology Fuller Theological Seminary Pasadena, California
Robert McAfee Brown	Emeritus Professor of Theology and Ethics Pacific School of Religion Berkeley, California
Eberhard Busch	Professor of Reformed Theology University of Göttingen Göttingen, West Germany
John Cobb	Professor of Theology School of Theology at Claremont Claremont, California
Arthur C. Cochrane	Emeritus Professor of Systematic Theology University of Dubuque Theological Seminary Dubuque, Iowa

Harvey Cox	Victor S. Thomas Professor of Divinity Harvard Divinity School Cambridge, Massachusetts
Langdon Gilkey	Shailer Mathews Professor of Theology University of Chicago Divinity School Chicago, Illinois
I. John Hesselink	Albertus C. Van Raalte Professor of Systematic Theology Western Theological Seminary Holland, Michigan
Paul Lehmann	Charles A. Briggs Professor of Systematic Theology, Emeritus Union Theological Seminary New York, New York
Martin E. Marty	Fairfax M. Cone Distinguished Service Professor of the History of Modern Christianity University of Chicago Divinity School Chicago, Illinois
Paul Minear	Winkley Professor of Biblical Theology Emeritus Yale University Divinity School New Haven, Connecticut
T. H. L. Parker	Sometime Vicar of Oakington, Rector of Great & Little Ponton, Vicar of Brothertoft Cambridge, England
Clark H. Pinnock	Professor of Theology McMaster Divinity College Hamilton, Ontario, Canada
Bernard L. Ramm	Pearl Rawlings Hamilton Professor of Christian Theology American Baptist Seminary of the West Berkeley, California
Dietrich Ritschl	Professor of Systematic Theology Director of the Ecumenical Institute

University of Heidelberg
Heidelberg, West Germany
Thomas F. Torrance   Professor of Dogmatics Emeritus
University of Edinburgh
Edinburgh, Scotland
Béla Vassady   Professor Emeritus of Systematic
Theology
Lancaster Theological Seminary
Lancaster, Pennsylvania
(Address: 2729 Leonard, NW, D-7
Grand Rapids, Michigan 49504)
Geoffrey Wainwright   Professor of Systematic Theology
Duke University
Durham, North Carolina
James A. Wharton   Perkins Professor of Homiletics
Perkins School of Theology
Southern Methodist University
Dallas, Texas
Michael Wyschogrod   Professor and Chairman
Department of Philosophy
Baruch College
The City University of New York
New York, New York
John Howard Yoder   Professor of Theology
University of Notre Dame
Notre Dame, Indiana

Chronology/Major Works

1886	Born in Basel
1904	University of Bern
1906	University of Berlin
1907	University of Tübingen
1908	University of Marburg
1908	Ordained
1909	Assistant Pastor in Geneva
1911	Pastor in Safenwil
1913	Marriage to Nelly Hoffmann
1919	First edition of *Der Römerbrief*
1921	Professor at Göttingen
1922	Second edition of *Der Römerbrief* (ET *The Epistle to the Romans*, 1935)
1922	Named Doctor of Theology by University of Münster
1924	*Das Wort Gottes und die Theologie* (ET *The Word of God and the Word of Man*, 1928)
1925	Professor at Münster
1928	*Prolegomena zur Christlichen Dogmatik*
1928	*Die Theologie und die Kirche* (ET *Theology and Church*, 1962)
1930	Professor at Bonn
1931	*Fides quaerens intellectum* (ET *Anselm: Fides quarens intellectum*, 1960)
1932	*Die Kirchliche Dogmatik* I/1 (ET *Church Dogmatics* I/1, 1936; rev. ed. 1975)
1933	*Theologische Existenz heute!* (ET *Theological Existence Today*, 1933)
1934	Barmen Synod and Declaration
1934	*Nein! Antwort an Emil Brunner* (ET in *Natural Theology*, 1946)
1935	Professor at Basel
1935	*Credo* (ET *Credo*, 1936)
1938	*Gotteserkenntnis und Gottesdienst* (ET *The Knowledge of God and the Service of God*, 1938)
1939	*Die Kirchliche Dogmatik* I/2 (ET *Church Dogmatics* I/2, 1956)
1940	*Die Kirchliche Dogmatik* II/1 (ET *Church Dogmatics* II/1, 1957)
1942	*Die Kirchliche Dogmatik* II/2 (ET *Church Dogmatics* II/2, 1957)

1943   *Die Kirchliche Lehre von der Taufe* (ET *The Teaching of the
       Church Regarding Baptism,* 1948)
1945   *Die Kirchliche Dogmatik* III/1 (ET *Church Dogmatics* III/1,
       1958)
1947   *Die protestantische Theologie im 19. Jahrhundert* (ET
       Protestant Theology in the Nineteenth Century, 1972)
1947   *Dogmatik im Grundriss* (ET *Dogmatics in Outline,* 1949)
1948   *Die Kirchliche Dogmatik* III/2 (ET *Church Dogmatics* III/2,
       1960)
1950   *Die Kirchliche Dogmatik* III/3 (ET *Church Dogmatics* III/3,
       1961)
1951   *Die Kirchliche Dogmatik* III/4 (ET *Church Dogmatics* III/4,
       1961)
1952   *Rudolf Bultmann. Ein Versuch, ihn zu verstehen* (ET "Rudolf
       Bultmann—An Attempt to Understand Him" in *Kerygma and
       Myth* II, 1962)
1953   *Die Kirchliche Dogmatik* IV/1 (ET *Church Dogmatics* IV/1,
       1956)
1954   *Against the Stream: Shorter Post-War Writings 1946–1952*
1955   *Die Kirchliche Dogmatik* IV/2 (ET *Church Dogmatics* IV/2,
       1958)
1956   *Die Menschlichkeit Gottes* (ET *The Humanity of God,* 1961)
1959   *Die Kirchliche Dogmatik* IV/3 pt. 1 (ET *Church Dogmatics*
       IV/3 pt. 1, 1961)
1959   *Die Kirchliche Dogmatik* IV/3 pt. 2 (ET *Church Dogmatics*
       IV/3 pt. 2, 1962)
1962   *Einfuhrung in die evangelische Theologie* (ET *Evangelical
       Theology,* 1963)
1967   *Die Kirchliche Dogmatik* IV/4 [fragment] (ET *Church
       Dogmatics* IV/4 [fragment], 1969)
1968   Death
1978   *Karl Barth: Die Theologie Schleiermachers* (ET *The Theology
       of Schleiermacher,* 1982)
1981   *Ethics* (Ger. *Ethik* I [1928] and *Ethik* II [1928-29])
1981   *Die Kirchliche Dogmatik* Lecture Fragments (ET *The Christian
       Life,* 1981)